C[OOKING WITH] WINE

FLAVORFUL RECIPES AND TIPS ON SERVING WINES WITH FOOD

CAMILLE STAGG

TIME® LIFE BOOKS

TIME-LIFE BOOKS, ALEXANDRIA, VIRGINIA

TIME-LIFE BOOKS IS A DIVISION OF TIME LIFE INC.

TIME-LIFE CUSTOM PUBLISHING

Vice President and Publisher	Terry Newell
Associate Publisher	Teresa Hartnett
Vice President of Sales and Marketing	Neil Levin
Project Manager	Jennifer Michelle Lee
Director of Special Sales	Liz Ziehl
Managing Editor	Donia Ann Steele
Director of Design	Christopher M. Register

First Printing. Printed in Canada

TIME-LIFE is a trademark of Time Warner Inc. U.S.A.

Produced by Storey Communications, Inc.,
105 Schoolhouse Road, Pownal, Vermont 05261

President	M. John Storey
Executive Vice President	Martha M. Storey
Vice President and Publisher	Pamela B. Art
Custom Publishing Director	Amanda R. Haar
Editors	Jeffrey D. Litton, Deirdre Lynch, and Angela Cardinali
Cover and Text Design	Black Trout Design, Carol J. Jessop
Text Production	Black Trout Design, Faith E. Kaufman
Illustrations	Laura Tedeschi, Leslie H. R. Noyes

Library of Congress Cataloging-in-Publication Data

Stagg, Camille J., 1942-
    Cooking with wine : flavorful recipes and tips on serving
wines / [by Camille Stagg].
        p.   cm.
    Includes index.
    ISBN 0-7835-4875-3
    1. Cookery (Wine)   I. Title.
    TX726.S7   1997
    641.6'22—dc21

                                        96-50878
                                        CIP

DEDICATION

I dedicate this book to my mother, Jeanette M. Stagg, a good cook who shared her kitchen with me and who instilled in me a lifelong interest in cooking, and to the memory of Tom Bentley, a friend of wine.

TABLE OF CONTENTS

ACKNOWLEDGMENTS

Many people deserve thanks for assisting with the research and compilation of this book.

A big special "thank you" to the students and recent graduates of Northwestern University's Medill School of Journalism who helped gather the current wine data, typed and edited copy and recipes, and offered computer advice. Key to this project was Amy Debra Feldman, who did all the above tasks as well as assisting with recipe testing. We worked many long days and evenings together and maintained a sense of humor until the deadline. Ritu Upadhyay, Adrienne Philia Samuels, and Lyle Sinrod Walter did a big share of the work. Journalist Rummana Hussain also was part of our team.

Joan Hersh, key recipe tester and developer for this book, is a pastry chef and proprietor of A Matter of Course, a Chicago catering firm. Susan Parent Runnion, also a recipe tester and developer for this book, is a graduate of the Cooking & Hospitality Institute of Chicago (CHIC).

Courtesy reviews of the manuscript and guidance were provided by Robert H. Bradford, Boston-based photojournalist, wine columnist and critic; John D. Davis, wine expert and owner and founder of A Taste of California, the largest wine-of-the-month club in the United States; Patrick Fegan, founder and director of the Chicago Wine School; Evan Goldstein, director of the Sterling Vineyards School of Service & Hospitality; Bob Rohden, President, Laserlist Chicago and a wine and computer consultant; and Barbara Sadek, food editor of the Chicago Sun-Times.

Special thanks as well to Ed Jarratt, for his office support, to Marylyn Seif, for her office assistance, and to attorney Lowell Komie, for his counsel.

I am grateful to all the wine experts, chefs, wineries, wine associations, distributors, consulate offices, and others who cooperated in sending me materials necessary to write this book. Many wonderful friends and neighbors were supportive and helpful throughout this project. I have been privileged to work with top editors at Storey Communications, Angela Cardinali, Deirdre Lynch, and Jeff Litton, who have given me ongoing guidance and support.

INTRODUCTION

USING WINE IN THE KITCHEN

Food and wine can be delicious on their own, but it's very exciting when a bite of food and a sip of wine intermingle in the mouth to create a wonderful new sensation. Something similar can happen in the pot or the bowl, when food and wine work together to create a better dish.

Wine enhances sauces, poaching liquids, bastes, marinades, dressings, and baked products. It can be used to baste, to deglaze a pan for a sauce, to macerate fruit, or as a soaking bath. Wine can add a subtle flavor note or forceful emphasis to a dish.

The intensity and taste of a wine's flavor changes depending on the cooking procedure. For example, when a little wine is added to a sauce at the end of cooking, it will retain most of its aroma and flavor. If it is simmered a long time, as in a stew, or given direct heat, many of the flavoring components evaporate, leaving a pleasantly bitter taste. When reduced to its essence, wine adds an intense, concentrated flavor to the dish. When sweet wines are flambéed, the sugar caramelizes and transforms to give a burnt-sugar taste. Since alcohol begins evaporating at its low boiling point of 172°F, there is no alcohol left in most cooked wine dishes.

The acids and tannins in wine—organic compounds from the skins and stems of the grape—tenderize tough meat cuts while imparting flavor. Since poultry and fish do not require tenderizing, they can be marinated for less time than red meat. The acid from wine reduces a meat's moisture retention capacity during cooking, so the meat might lose some juices but it gains tenderness and flavor from the marination.

PAIRING WINE WITH FOOD

Traditionally there have been strict guidelines about food and wine matching, especially the well-worn "white with fish and chicken and red with meat." However, the tendency in recent years has been to experiment more and avoid restrictions, to relax and experience various global cuisines. Experimenting and tasting is a fun learning process, so don't be afraid to make some mistakes.

We do want happy matches at the table, and are looking for wines that don't conflict with the foods we serve. For the most harmonious dining, consider the following basic principles of wine and food compatibility.

SIMILARITIES Wine and food can be similar in elemental tastes, flavors, intensity, and texture. By pairing wines with food to match one or all of these characteristics, you can create winning combinations.

A crisp Pinot Grigio or Sauvignon Blanc with chicken in a citrus sauce emphasizes the tartness in both the wine and the sauce. A spicy Gewürztraminer wine can accommodate most spicy foods (Thai or Szechwan). However, high-alcohol wines, such as some Chardonnays, unpleasantly intensify the heat in chilies and should be avoided.

Wines that are in step with the robustness of the food, such as a full-bodied Cabernet Sauvignon, go well with hearty dishes such as lamb stew. Match wines and foods that are similar in intensity so neither overpowers the other. For instance, a delicate scallop dish is complemented by a light Riesling or Chenin Blanc.

OPPOSITES Chinese cuisine takes advantage of the principle of opposites. Try pairing some foods with wines of contrasting taste, flavor, and texture for a similar palate-pleasing effect. An example of a sweet/sour combination is a fruity Riesling with a fish in a tart sorrel sauce. For a sweet/salty pairing, try slightly sweet wines such as semidry Riesling, a soft Chenin Blanc, or a fruity Gamay Beaujolais with salty foods. The sour/salty contrast also works. Acidic wines such as Pinot Grigio and Pinot Blanc, or a dry Champagne, usually pair best with the saltiness of caviar.

Another contrast that works is a less acidic food with a more acidic wine. For instance, the richness of a creamy sauce is best cut with a crisp, tart white wine such as certain

Sauvignon Blancs or crisp Champagnes. Also, acidic white wines such as Pinot Blanc and dry Champagnes or sparkling wines cut the richness of a dish that is fried or prepared in a cream sauce.

BALANCE The fruit/acid balance in a wine provides its character and definition. For the full flavor of a wine to come through, the sweetness or tartness of a dish should be less intense than that of the wine. For example, a dry Chardonnay can be wonderful with chicken cooked in an apple or pear sauce, but it would be overpowered by a sweet fruit tart. However, sweeter wines and foods neutralize each other. Serve dessert wines as sweet as the dessert, or the sweet food will make the wine taste bitter.

Bitter taste comes into play with the more tannic red wines, which are compatible with fattier foods. The fat coats the tongue and defuses the bitterness, so the fat and the bitter make a happy marriage. The exception here is fatty fish, since the fish oils do not mask the bitterness of tannins.

TEXTURE Foods and wines have textures that affect compatibility. Some wines are thin, light, and crisp; others are more chewy, buttery, and robust. A dry, light wine and a crisp, sparkling wine are both refreshing on the tongue and cleanse the palate nicely when eaten with fatty food or a rich, thick sauce.

MAJOR WINE CLASSIFICATIONS

Wines are generally organized into the following basic categories: table wines (white, red, and rosé), aperitif, dessert, and sparkling wines.

White table wines are fermented without grape skins, and range in color from pale straw to deep golden. They have more natural grape acids than red wines and sharper flavor. They are usually best served chilled. Red table wines are completely fermented with grape skins, and can be light red to deep garnet and purple. Rosés generally are partially fermented with skins, and can be a blend of white and red; they are pink or pale peach-hued. Reds are served at cool room temperature and rosés are served chilled.

Apéritif and dessert wines share many similarities. They tend to be higher in alcohol content than table and sparkling wines and are more assertively flavored. Some main aperitif selections are: French dry vermouth, Dubonnet, Lillet, Italian marsala, sweet vermouth, and Spanish sherries such as fino, manzanilla, and Amontillado.

Key dessert wines are Portuguese Madeira and port (ruby and tawny), Spanish oloroso or sweet cream sherry, Italian marsala, Muscat (also Moscato in Italy), French Sauternes, and Hungarian Tokaji (Tokay, Hungary's strong, sweet wine).

Sparkling wines are spirited and cele-bratory. We often mistakenly call all sparkling wines champagne. However, Champagne is produced exclusively in the Champagne province of northern France. These strictly con-trolled wines are made by a specific process, méthode cham-penoise. All other are simply sparkling wines, and are made in many countries, including the United States. Other foreign sparklers are Spanish cava, German sekt, and Italian spumante.

Following is a list of the most well-known grape varieties with some proven food matches.

Whites

CHARDONNAY. (shar-doh-nay) Many experts say this is the finest of all dry white wine grapes, important in France and in California, and now planted around the world. These wines are medium- to full-bodied with styles rang-ing from crisp and clean to oak-aged, robust, and com-plex. Aromas and flavors: apple, ripe fig, buttery, toasty.

Food Matches: medium to heartier fish and seafood, poul-try, and pork preparations.

CHENIN BLANC. (sheh-nan blahn) Main white grape of the mid-Loire region of France (e.g. Vouvray) and popular in California, where it is usually made soft and slightly sweet and light- to medium-bodied. Can be made dry. Aroma and flavors: citrus, apple, floral.

Food Matches: simple or slightly spicy fish, shellfish; poultry, veal, and pork items; bratwurst.

GEWÜRZTRAMINER. (ge-vurtz-tra-mee-ner) Spiciest of the wine grapes. Wines are often rich and soft, even when dry. Alsace makes the best and probably the driest; also made in Germany, eastern Europe, California (where it tends to be sweeter), and Australia. Aroma can be perfumey. Cinnamon and sweet spice, lychee fruit, rose characteristics.

Food Matches: spicier fish, poultry, pork, sausage, and vegetable items; lightly smoked foods.

PINOT BLANC. (pee-no blahn) Medium-bodied, crisp, dry. Similar to Chardonnay without the complexity and intensity. Grown in Champagne, Alsace, Germany, eastern Europe, Italy, and California. Floral bouquet; peach tones.

Food Matches: lightly seasoned fish, poultry, and vegetables; cream sauces.

PINOT GRIS. (pee-no gree) Known as Pinot Grigio in Italy where they tend to be crisp and dry. Also called Tokay d'Alsace and Rulander in Germany. Hints of fresh grape; gives full white wines.

Food Matches: light or tart fish, shellfish, and poultry; vegetables in a creamy sauce.

RIESLING. (reece-ling) Also Johannisberg, Rhine, or White Riesling. Germany's most noble grape; yields Rhine and Moselle wines. Grown in many places, including France, eastern Europe, Australia, South Africa, and California. Makes dry or sweet wines. Excellent sweet/acid balance. Light- to medium-bodied. Can be flowery when young and subtle and complex when mature. Aroma and taste: green apples, peaches, floral, honey.

Food Matches: delicate shellfish and fish; seasoned chicken, Cornish hen, turkey, sausages, and vegetables.

SAUVIGNON BLANC. (so-veen-yohn blahn) Also known as fumé blanc. Medium-bodied, popular white wine grape; when blended with Semillon, can produce the finest white Bordeaux. The dry California versions have become the second most popular white wine after Chardonnay. Aroma and flavors: herbaceous, grassy, often smoky; lively herb or melon.

Food Matches: smoked fish or poultry; white-fleshed fish; fish or poultry with rich buttery or creamy sauces.

SEMILLON. (sem-ee-yohn) Medium- to full-bodied. Contributes to the richness of fine French sweet Sauternes. Component of French dry white Graves. Wines are ambrosial and traditionally dry. In certain conditions, the grape can get "noble rot," which produces luscious sweet wines. Aromas of citrus and apricots.

Food Matches: lighter shellfish; more delicate fish; simply prepared poultry.

Reds

BARBERA. (bar-bear-uh) Medium-bodied. One of the grapes of Piemonte in Italy; grows well in California. Produces dark, medium-to-full, forward-fruity wine balanced with high acidity. Aroma and taste of berries and plums.

Food Matches: heartily flavored lamb chops; steaks; venison; sausages.

CABERNET FRANC. (cab-er-nay franc) Medium-bodied; lean; low in tannin. Associated mostly with Bordeaux and Loire wines of France. Also planted in Italy. In California it is mostly blended with Cabernet Sauvignon. Produces wines similar to Cabernet Sauvignon but lighter. Aroma of herbs and raspberries.

Food Matches: roasted beef or pork; grilled pork chops; duck.

CABERNET SAUVIGNON. (cab-er-nay so-veen-yohn) Rich and full-bodied. Great French red Bordeaux grape that is the backbone of the best wines of that region. Highly tannic; produces complex wines of longevity. Yields some of the finest red wines of California. Styles vary. Aroma and flavors of green peppers, plums, black currants, and often mint and eucalyptus.

Food Matches: grilled or roasted lamb; also herbed beef steaks and roasts; venison.

GAMAY. (gam-may) Light, lively, fruity; the French Gamay grape makes charming, fragrant wines, including the Beaujolais Nouveau, that are at their best when young and chilled.
Food Matches: white meats, poultry; bold Mediterranean flavors of garlic and olives.

GAMAY BEAUJOLAIS. (gam-may boh-zho-lay) Light, fresh, and fruity; the American Gamay Beaujolais is a Pinot Noir variety grown in California, not the true Gamay of France; strawberries and cherries in the nose and taste; can be served chilled.
Food Matches: a good summer wine with lighter meats (pork, veal, poultry); duck with sweeter bastes; marinated grilled vegetables; Mediterranean dishes.

GRENACHE. (gren-nahsh) Medium-bodied; forward fruit; little tannin. Popular in southern France. Also in Spain (garnacha), California, and Australia. Blackberries and other berries, cherries; smooth taste.
Food Matches: spicy poultry and barbecued ribs; pork and poultry with sweet bastes; Mediterranean dishes.

MERLOT. (mare-lo) Medium- to full-bodied; softer tannins and shorter-lived than Cabernet Sauvignon, with which it's often blended. Important in Bordeaux for contributing mellowness and suppleness to wines. Also key in California, where it is currently gaining popularity, as well as Chile, Argentina, and Australia. Plums and herbs in aroma; smooth, velvety taste.
Food Matches: grilled tuna steaks; beef steaks; baby lamb chops; herbed beef.

NEBBIOLO. (ne-bee-oh-lo) Full-bodied, this noble Italian wine grape is among the world's best. One of the two main indigenous red wine grapes of Italy, the other being Sangiovese. It grows best on steep hillsides, such as those of Piemonte. It is now also grown in California. Produces Barolo and Barbaresco wines, and generally sturdy wines high in tannin and alcohol that usually require considerable aging. Fully mature wines are rich and can be of world-class quality. Deep fruit aroma and full taste.

Food Matches: roast beef and venison; broiled or grilled steaks; richer pastas and risottos.

PETITE SIRAH. (puh-teet see-rah) Full-bodied, red wine grape that was thought to be Syrah of northern Rhône Valley in France, and therefore so-named in California. Later it was identified as another variety from southern France that is no longer grown there. Quantities have diminished in California, and most of the tannic, deep-colored wine has been used for blending with light wines. As a varietal, it is peppery and spicy in aroma and taste and improves with age.

Food Matches: seasoned Cornish hen and turkey; barbecued meats; lamb.

PINOT NOIR. (pee-no nwhar) Medium- to full-bodied and rich. Distinguished French red grape that is widely planted in France, especially in Burgundy and Champagne. Also popular worldwide. It does well in cooler climates of California and is widely planted in Oregon. Produces all of the great red Burgundies and some of the méthode champenoise sparkling wines. It produces wine with aromas and flavors of black cherries, raspberries, and strawberries.

Food Matches: grilled salmon and swordfish steaks; pork and veal chops; duck and game birds.

SANGIOVESE. (san-joh-vaz-zeh) Medium-bodied, this is one of the two most important red grapes native to Italy, where it is planted around the country. The main grape of Tuscany; it is the main variety in Chianti, which can range from light and fresh to a full, mature riserva. It also yields some of Italy's wine of longevity, such as Brunello. Rich, deep berry aromas and flavor tones.

Food Matches: spicy tomato-sauced pastas; fully seasoned veal, pork, and chicken; lighter red meats.

SYRAH. (see-rah) Full-bodied, rich, tannic northern Rhône Valley grape that yields some excellent wines, such as Côte Rotie and red wines of Hermitage. Popular in Australia, where it is called Shiraz or Hermitage. Small amount in California. Hints of blueberries, black pepper, and sometimes herbs.

Food Matches: richer meat and game dishes; duck preparations that are not sweet.

ZINFANDEL. (zin-fan-dell) Medium- to full-bodied, rich; good amount of tannin. Very popular and plentiful in California, which is about the only place it is planted. Comes from an unidentified grape thought to be Italian. Produces a wide range of styles including some great, intense wines. Aromas of spices, blackberries, black cherries; can be herbaceous.

Food Matches: spicy and barbecued meats and poultry; duck with fruity marinades; spicy pastas; tuna and swordfish steaks.

A NOTE FROM THE AUTHOR

Most of these recipes were fashioned around a particular style of wine as the focal point. In addition to my own creations, I am pleased to include some wonderful recipes from chefs and other experts in the wine field who were willing to share their culinary secrets.

I've made these recipes as healthful as possible. Recipes are trimmed of excess fat and sugar, and healthful cooking methods are emphasized. Canola or olive oil is the main fat used. Very little butter and cream is used, except when important to preserve the character of the dish. Fresh produce is used abundantly, and I've relied on wine, fresh herbs, and other seasonings for flavoring. The simplest recipes are at the start of each chapter.

The pairings are mostly general, except in some cases where I recommend specific wines I've enjoyed. Refer to the recommended wine list (see Appendix B, p.134) for more wine selections. The wines I've screened are from all over the world and include mostly very good values.

May these wine recipes further your joy of cooking!

"Good wine is a good familiar creature if it be well used."

William Shakespeare

CHAPTER 1
APPETIZERS AND FIRST COURSES

The recipes in this chapter were designed for typical apéritif wines such as brut Champagne and other dry sparkling wines, dry and fruitier whites, and light reds. Fortified wines, such as dry vermouth, Madeira, and sherries, are also good with finger foods. Wines that enrich the dish as an ingredient can be served along with it, but in several recipes such wines may be a bit heavy on the palate after one small glass.

PORT-BLUE CHEESE "CAKE" APPETIZER

At a press conference many years ago at the Biltmore Hotel in Los Angeles, I enjoyed a Stilton cheese appetizer. I asked the chef how he made it and was shocked to learn how simple it was. Since Stilton usually comes in huge wheels, I have made it several times with smaller rounds of other blue-veined cheeses. This recipe is a great addition to a wine-tasting party (see Appendix A, p. 132).

1 round (about 2–2½ pounds) blue cheese
⅔–1 cup ruby port
Toasted baguette slices or Italian bread

1. Poke 10–14 holes in the cheese round with a bamboo skewer or chopstick.

2. Pour port into the holes, being careful not to let any overflow.

3. Cover the cheese and let it stand at room temperature for at least 1–2 hours, or cover and refrigerate it overnight. Bring it to room temperature before serving with baguette slices or Italian bread. Leftover cheese may be covered and refrigerated for several weeks.

YIELD: 16–20 2-ounce appetizer servings
PAIRING: Brut Champagne or dry sparkling wine, Semillon, Gamay, or Port

ROASTED GARLIC GORGONZOLA PORT SPREAD

Once when I had garlic roasting in the oven and gorgonzola on hand, I decided to combine the two, then added some port and cream cheese to bind it. It was one of the best cheese spreads I ever ate, and I'm pleased to be able to share this recipe with you.

1 8-ounce package light cream cheese,
at room temperature
4 ounces gorgonzola, at room temperature, crumbled
3–4 tablespoons tawny port
3 cloves roasted garlic, mashed
Toasted melba rounds, whole wheat pita wedges,
or crusty baguette slices

1. In a blender or medium bowl, combine cream cheese and gorgonzola, mixing to blend a bit. Add port and mix thoroughly. Add garlic and mix well.

2. Cover and let stand for 30 minutes, or refrigerate for at least 1 hour for flavors to blend.

3. Serve with melba rounds, pita bread, or baguettes.

YIELD: Makes 6–12 appetizer servings
PAIRING: Tawny port, dry Riesling, or dry Spumante

WINE CHEESE SPREAD

This cheese spread is a delicious party snack. It's quick and easy to make and can be stored in the refrigerator until you're ready to serve it. Keep some on hand for those impromptu holiday get-togethers. Serve at room temperature on plain crackers, and sip wine along with it.

$\frac{1}{2}$ pound shredded medium-sharp Cheddar or Herkimer,
at room temperature
$\frac{1}{2}$ pound shredded Fontina or Jarlsberg,
at room temperature
3 tablespoons softened butter or margarine
$\frac{1}{3}$ cup light red wine (Pinot Noir or Grenache)
2 tablespoons brandy
4 ounces softened light cream cheese or
Neufchâtel cheese
Plain crackers or toasted pita bread wedges

1. Blend half the cream cheese with the remaining ingredients, except crackers, in a food processor or blender until smooth.

2. Gradually add enough of the remaining cream cheese to make the mixture smooth and spreadable.

3. Pack the blended cheese into a 1-pint serving bowl, cover, and refrigerate for at least a day to allow the flavors to blend. Serve at room temperature with crackers. This spread keeps well for six to eight weeks if properly refrigerated.

YIELD: About 2 cups
PAIRING: Dry white wine such as Pinot Blanc or Sauvignon Blanc; lighter dry red wines such as
Pinot Noir, Merlot, or some Zinfandels

SAUVIGNON BLANC CEVICHE

In this classic Mexican dish, the lime juice and wine marinate the fish and eliminate the need for cooking. This version is a delicious combination of turbot, tomatoes, onions, chilies, and cilantro. It can be prepared a day in advance of serving and, since it requires no cooking, makes a good appetizer or first course, particularly on hot days.

1¾ pounds turbot fillets, cut into ¾-inch cubes

⅓ cup Sauvignon Blanc

⅓ cup lime juice

2 tablespoons diced canned green chilies, drained

1 small onion, chopped

2 medium plum tomatoes, peeled and chopped

3 tablespoons olive oil

¼ cup chopped fresh or 1½ teaspoons dried cilantro leaves

1 teaspoon salt

Garnish: cilantro sprigs

1. Combine fish, wine, and lime juice in a shallow glass dish. Cover and refrigerate, stirring occasionally, until the fish becomes opaque. Refrigerate at least 8 hours or preferably overnight.

2. Combine chilies, onion, tomatoes, oil, cilantro, and salt in a bowl. Stir into the fish mixture. Cover and refrigerate for 1 hour before serving. Spoon into individual small bowls or cups, garnish each with a cilantro sprig, and serve cold.

YIELD: 10–12 servings as an appetizer
PAIRING: Sauvignon Blanc, Pinot Blanc, or Pinot Grigio

MADEIRA-LIVER PÂTÉ

This deliciously simple pâté is sure to be a hit at your next party. Braunschweiger is used to save time and labor over the from-scratch version where the liver must be cleaned, cooked, and puréed. The mushrooms with a medium-dry Madeira add a double kiss of flavor, and the sour cream contributes a rich, velvety texture. Serve with apéritif wines, such as dry Champagne and sparkling wines, or dry white wines. A dry Madeira will bridge the flavor to the Madeira in the pâté.

1 tablespoon butter or margarine
$\frac{1}{4}$ pound mushrooms, sliced
1 tablespoon chopped green onions
$\frac{1}{2}$ pound braunschweiger, peeled and cut into chunks
(liverwurst or liver sausage found in some markets can be used)
$\frac{1}{2}$ cup sour cream (low-fat sour cream may be substituted)
2–2$\frac{1}{2}$ tablespoons medium-dry Madeira
$\frac{1}{2}$ teaspoon Dijon mustard
Dash of cayenne
Garnish: Snipped parsley and 1 parsley sprig
Melba rounds or baguette slices

1. Melt butter in a medium sauté pan over medium-high heat until foam subsides. Add the mushrooms and cook for about 2 minutes until soft. Place the mushrooms and remaining ingredients in the bowl of a food processor and blend until smooth.

2. Transfer the mixture to a serving bowl. Cover and refrigerate for a few hours or overnight. Garnish the pâté with parsley and serve with melba rounds or baguette slices.

YIELD: 2 cups or about 32 appetizer rounds
PAIRING: Dry Madeira, Champagne, or Pinot Blanc

WINE-MINT MARINATED MINI-BEEF PATTIES

This wine-mint marinade for beef patties can be used for mini-lamb patties as well; simply adjust the other flavorings to suit your taste. Increasing the amount of garlic and Dijon mustard, for example, will produce a more piquant flavor.

1½ pounds lean ground beef
½ cup medium-bodied dry red wine
(Cabernet Sauvignon, Merlot, or Zinfandel)
2 tablespoons olive oil
1 tablespoon Dijon mustard
1 medium clove garlic, crushed
1 tablespoon plus 1 teaspoon minced fresh parsley
1 tablespoon minced fresh or ¾ teaspoon dried mint leaves
Freshly ground black pepper

1. Divide meat into 12 equal portions. Shape each portion into a patty and arrange all in a shallow glass or nonmetal pan.

2. To make the marinade, combine wine with remaining ingredients in a glass measuring cup. Pour it over the patties, turning the meat to coat both sides. Marinate for 15–30 minutes, turning once.

3. Preheat broiler. Drain patties, reserving the marinade. Place patties on the broiler pan and cook several inches from the heat for about 3 minutes, until brown. Turn and baste them with the marinade. Continue broiling the patties for about 3 minutes, basting with remaining marinade, until the meat is browned and medium-rare.

YIELD: 12 2-ounce appetizer servings
PAIRING: Smooth medium-bodied Cabernet Sauvignon, Merlot, or Zinfandel

POLENTA
TRIANGLES

Polenta, Italian cuisine's version of cornmeal, is very versatile. For this recipe, a dry Italian white wine replaces some of the usual water. The various toppings to the finished polenta provide flavor components that are key in determining wine pairings. Experiment with different toppings and offer several to your guests.

1 cup dry Italian white wine (Pinot Grigio)

2 cups water

1 teaspoon salt

1 large clove garlic, minced

1 tablespoon chopped fresh
or $\frac{3}{4}$ teaspoon dried oregano

$\frac{1}{2}$ small onion, finely minced

1 cup coarse cornmeal (special high-priced 'polenta' is not necessary; Quaker cornmeal or any other domestic brand is fine)

6–8 ounces Fontina cheese, shredded

Some topping options: roasted red peppers, chopped olives, green pepper slices, thinly sliced prosciutto, Fresh-Tomato Wine Sauce (see p. 106), Wild Mushroom Sauce (see p. 104), and leftover Thirty-Minute Turkey Chili (see p. 23).

1. Bring wine and water to a boil in a heavy, medium-sized saucepan. Add salt, garlic, oregano, and onion and simmer for 5 minutes.

2. Add the cornmeal very slowly, picking it up a handful at a time and letting it dribble through your fingers into the pot, stirring constantly with either a wooden spoon or a wooden-handled whisk. The polenta will take about 20 minutes to cook and it must be stirred almost constantly to prevent lumps.

The whisk works well for this and the spoon helps to scrape the bottom and sides of the pot, so both are recommended.

3. When the polenta is very thick, after 20 minutes, pour and spread evenly onto a greased cookie sheet to cool. Refrigerate for at least 2 hours, or until firm. Cut into small triangles, add cheese and the other toppings, except the sauces or chili, which are best heated separately and spooned over the polenta.

4. Bake in preheated 350°F oven until the cheese melts, about 10 minutes.

5. For finger food, serve polenta with toppings on small plates. (You may need forks, since polenta is soft when warm and can be messy.) As a first or side course, serve polenta with a tomato or mushroom sauce, or the turkey chili.

YIELD: Approximately 30 appetizer triangles
PAIRING: Pinot Grigio or Sauvignon Blanc

"There are more old wine
drinkers than old doctors."

German Proverb

CHAPTER 2
SALADS, SOUPS, AND STEWS

Many soups, cold or hot, benefit from the addition of wine, which can take the place of some of the broth. Similarly, adding wine instead of vinegar to a dressing ensures that the salad will be wine-friendly and will not "argue" with a wine at dinner. The soups and salads in this chapter, which use different styles of wine, will enhance your dinner menus.

ASIAN GREEN AND WHITE SALAD

This is a lovely salad to look at as well as eat. The green and white tones please the eye, and the full flavors of sesame oil, semidry white wine, garlic, and fresh ginger please the palate. It has loads of texture and is most refreshing.

$2\frac{1}{2}$ tablespoons canola oil

1 tablespoon sesame oil

$\frac{1}{3}$ cup semidry white wine (Chenin Blanc or Semillon)

2 tablespoons rice vinegar

1 tablespoon minced fresh ginger

10 leaves Asian basil, finely chopped

1 tablespoon crushed garlic

8 ounces firm tofu, drained and diced

$1\frac{1}{2}$ cups coarsely shredded Romaine lettuce

$1\frac{1}{2}$ cups coarsely shredded Napa Chinese cabbage

3 green onions, sliced

$1\frac{1}{2}$ cups seeded and thinly sliced (1-inch strips)
green bell pepper,

2 ounces fresh water chestnuts, peeled and sliced

1. Combine canola and sesame oils, wine, rice vinegar, ginger, basil, and garlic in a shallow glass dish or container. Stir. Let stand for 15 minutes for flavors to blend. Add tofu and marinate for 15 minutes.

2. Combine lettuce, cabbage, green onions, bell pepper, and water chestnuts in a large bowl. Transfer marinated tofu and dressing onto the salad. Toss gently and serve.

YIELD: 4 servings as a side dish; 2 servings
as a main course
PAIRING: Dry Riesling or Sauvignon Blanc

THIRTY-MINUTE TURKEY CHILI

This quick chili is so delicious, it's as if it had simmered for hours. For the chili peppers, try ancho, guajillo, or pequin, rather than the more common mixture sold in supermarkets as "chili powder." This is a great all-in-one meal, made healthful with turkey instead of red meat, and enhanced with wine.

1–1½ pounds ground turkey (15% fat)

3 medium onions, chopped

4 garlic cloves, minced

1 red bell pepper, diced

2 tablespoons assorted ground chili peppers

½ teaspoon ground cumin

½ cup Cabernet Sauvignon

2 9-ounce cans of whole or diced tomatoes

6-ounce can of tomato paste

¼ cup hot salsa (or to taste)

2 15-ounce cans of beans (pinto, kidney, red, pink, or black), drained and rinsed

1 15-ounce can of corn, drained and rinsed

1. In a large saucepan, brown turkey over medium heat for 5 minutes, breaking it apart as it cooks. Add onions, garlic, and red pepper; cook for 10 minutes.

2. Add chili peppers, cumin, wine, tomatoes, tomato paste, and salsa. Bring to a boil over medium-high heat, stirring often. Then lower the heat so the chili simmers, and cook for 10 minutes.

3. Add beans and corn, cooking for 5 minutes or until mixture bubbles. Serve over squares of hot cornbread or polenta in a soup bowl.

YIELD: 4 servings
PAIRING: A mellow Cabernet Sauvignon or Merlot from California or a sturdy white wine, such as a Chardonnay

DILLED POTATO-LEEK RIESLING SOUP

The classic vichyssoise is a wonderful cold French soup made of potatoes, leeks, milk, and cream. Three of these compatible elements have been adapted to this soup, embellished with a semidry Riesling. Serve it hot with crusty bread for a very satisfying lunch or first course.

5 medium Yukon Gold potatoes (1$\frac{1}{4}$ pounds), scrubbed, peeled, and cut into $\frac{1}{2}$-inch cubes

2 medium leeks, rinsed thoroughly and cut into $\frac{1}{2}$-inch dice

1 small onion, finely chopped

1$\frac{3}{4}$ cups semidry Riesling

1$\frac{1}{2}$ cups water

$\frac{1}{2}$ teaspoon salt

10 grinds black pepper

1$\frac{1}{2}$ cups milk (whole or 2%)

2$\frac{1}{2}$–3 tablespoons fresh dill, minced

1. In a medium saucepan, combine potatoes, leeks, onion, wine, water, salt, and pepper. Bring to a boil, then lower heat. Cover and simmer for 50 minutes.

2. In a food processor, purée soup in batches, then return to saucepan.

3. Stir in milk and dill. Bring to a simmer over low heat but do not boil. Serve, adding salt and pepper to taste.

YIELD: 4–6 servings
PAIRING: Dry Riesling or Sauvignon Blanc

THREE GREENS GOAT CHEESE SALAD
with 1-2-3 Vermouth Dressing

This salad is quick and easy to prepare. The addition of the vermouth dressing makes it an elegant appetizer.

1-2-3 Vermouth Dressing (see recipe below)
4 ounces fresh goat cheese (chèvre), in 4 even slices
1 quart mixed torn greens (Romaine, red leaf lettuce,
and curly endive are good choices)
8 medium button mushrooms, sliced
8 medium radishes, sliced

1. Make 1-2-3 Vermouth Dressing. Marinate goat cheese in 2 tablespoons of the dressing for 30 minutes–1 hour.

2. Arrange mixed greens on each of the four salad plates. Top each with one slice of the marinated goat cheese. Divide mushrooms and radishes among the four plates and serve with the remaining dressing.

YIELD: 4 servings
PAIRING: Pinot Grigio or Grenache

1-2-3 VERMOUTH DRESSING
1 tablespoon sweet vermouth
2-3 tablespoons dry vermouth, or slightly more to taste
3 tablespoons light olive oil
Fresh lime juice to taste (about 1 tablespoon)
Salt and freshly ground black pepper to taste

1. Blend vermouths and olive oil with lime juice in a glass measuring cup. Add salt and pepper to taste.

YIELD: About $\frac{1}{2}$ cup dressing

WINTER SQUASH SOUP

Winter squash has a natural sweetness that is enhanced by a semidry white wine. Fragrant with ginger and nutmeg, the soup is somehow sweeter-tasting without the thyme. I like it both ways.

1 pound winter squash (acorn or butternut),
halved lengthwise
1 red bell pepper
2 cups chicken or vegetable broth
1 tablespoon olive oil
1 heaping teaspoon freshly grated ginger
1 medium onion, diced
$\frac{1}{2}$ cup semidry white wine (Semillon or Riesling)
$\frac{1}{2}$ teaspoon freshly grated nutmeg
1 teaspoon minced fresh thyme
or $\frac{1}{4}$ teaspoon dried thyme
$\frac{1}{2}$ teaspoon salt
Freshly ground black pepper to taste

1. Cook the squash in either a preheated 375°F oven or a microwave. If using an oven, place squash cut-side down in a pan filled with $\frac{1}{2}$-inch water. Roast until very tender, 45–60 minutes. If using a microwave, wrap each half of the squash tightly in a piece of microwave-proof plastic wrap. Cook on high for 8 minutes. Cool, seed, scoop out flesh, and set aside.

2. While the squash is cooking, roast the pepper. If using a gas stove, put the pepper directly over a high flame, turning as each side blackens. If using a broiler, preheat it to 425°F. Slice the pepper in half through the stem and flatten each piece. Place the pepper on a piece of aluminum foil on the broiler's middle shelf and cook for 10–15 minutes, turning on all sides until blackened.

3. Remove blackened pepper from heat and let cool in a paper bag for about 15 minutes. Peel (skin will slip off), seed, and purée in a blender or food processor with several tablespoons of broth, taken from the 2 cups called for in the recipe. Set aside.

4. Heat the oil over low heat in a $2\frac{1}{2}$-quart saucepan. Add the ginger and onion and cook for 15 minutes over low heat. Add the wine, increase the heat, and boil until the mixture is reduced by about half. This will take 3–5 minutes.

5. Transfer the onion mixture to a blender or food processor. Add the cooked squash, remaining broth, nutmeg, thyme, and salt. Purée until smooth.

6. Transfer the soup back to the pan and heat for a few minutes. Remove from heat and serve immediately, topping each portion with a spoonful of the pepper purée. Add black pepper to taste.

YIELD: 4 servings
PAIRING: Pinot Blanc, Pinot Grigio, or Gamay Beaujolais

CHICKEN NIÇOISE STYLE

Niçoise salad is a classic from the south of France. Instead of tuna, this version uses chicken, and regular green beans are used instead of the tiny French green beans, haricots verts. Kalamata olives are substituted for the hard-to-find Niçoise olives. The White Wine Dressing makes this salad compatible with wine served at a dinner.

¾ pound small new potatoes, cut into 2-inch wedges
½ pound fresh green beans, cut into 2-inch lengths
1 tablespoon canola oil
1 skinless, boneless chicken breast, cut into
2 x ½-inch pieces
½ pound cherry tomatoes, halved
⅛ pound pitted Kalamata olives,
cut into quarters lengthwise
White Wine Dressing (see recipe at right)
16 leaves of Romaine or other crisp salad greens, torn
into bite-size pieces

1. Cook potatoes in a medium saucepan over medium-high heat for 2 minutes in boiling, salted water.

2. Add the green beans to potatoes and cook 5 minutes, or until potatoes and beans are tender. Drain and run under cold water, then set aside.

3. In a small skillet, heat the oil over medium-high heat. Add the chicken and sauté until cooked through, about 2 minutes per side.

4. Assemble the salad by tossing all the ingredients except salad greens in the dressing. Serve on the crisp greens on individual salad plates.

YIELD: 4 servings
PAIRING: Chenin Blanc or dry Riesling

WHITE WINE DRESSING

$\frac{1}{4}$ cup extra virgin olive oil

$\frac{1}{3}$ cup white wine

1 teaspoon lemon juice

$\frac{1}{4}$ teaspoon Dijon mustard

1 clove garlic, crushed

$\frac{1}{4}$ teaspoon chopped fresh basil

Salt and pepper to taste

1. To make the salad dressing, add all the ingredients in a small covered container and shake well.

CHILLED CRANBERRY BORSCHT

I grew up loving my mother's Polish beet borscht. One type was served hot with beet chunks, and another variation was a clear broth served chilled. Each was usually topped with a generous dollop of sour cream. This version, which pays respect to borscht's Eastern European roots, combines three red ingredients: beets, cranberry juice, and red wine. The beets are diced to give texture. It can be prepared a day ahead if your schedule is tight. Citrus and honey complete the happy picture and provide your taste buds with a sweet-tart taste. This soup needs no pairing because the meal's main course will determine the wine to be served.

4 small beets

3 cups cranberry juice

2 cups light red wine (Chianti, Gamay Beaujolais, or Grenache)

$\frac{1}{2}$ cup orange juice

Zest and juice from 1 orange

Zest and juice from 1 lime

2 tablespoons honey

4–5 tablespoons plain yogurt

1. Preheat oven to 350°F. Scrub the beets, but don't remove their ends. Wrap beets tightly together or individually in aluminum foil and bake for about 1 hour, or until they are easily pierced with a paring knife. Remove them from the oven and when completely cooled, cut off ends and remove skin. You should be able to do this easily with your fingers; if not, use a potato peeler. Dice the beets.

2. Place beets, cranberry juice, wine, orange and lime zest and juice, and honey in a medium saucepan (avoid aluminum pans if possible) over medium heat. Bring to a boil, lower heat, and simmer for 15 minutes. Remove from heat and cool to room temperature, then chill for at least 2 hours.

3. Divide soup into six bowls and add a dollop of yogurt to each before serving.

YIELD: 6 servings

CRANBERRY WINE PUNCH

Another version of this soup makes a deliciously different hot punch for a cold winter's night, and may be served with appetizers before a meal.

1. Prepare the borscht as described above, eliminating the beets and yogurt. Simmer the other ingredients as instructed and serve in six insulated mugs.

PORK GRENACHE STEW

This recipe was inspired by a stew made by my longtime friends Hedda Lubin and Gary Houston, who host a pumpkin party each fall. The star of their buffet is a pumpkin filled with a delectable, spicy meat stew, which changes slightly each year, and for which there is no set recipe. This variation is made with acorn squash, which is more readily available than pumpkin, and with pork instead of beef. For a vegetarian stew, omit the meat and reduce the water by half.

1⅓ pounds boneless pork, cut into 1-inch cubes (beef or lamb may be substituted)

1 tablespoon corn or canola oil

2 large carrots, scrubbed and sliced 1-inch thick

2 ears of corn, kernels cut off the cob

3–4 medium onions, coarsely chopped

3 medium parsnips, peeled and cut into 1-inch slices

24 dried apricot halves

Heaping ½ teaspoon ground cinnamon

⅔ cup water

1⅔ cups fruity red wine (Grenache or Gamay Beaujolais)

1 tablespoon honey, or to taste

2 medium acorn squash, halved lengthwise and seeded

8 small red potatoes, scrubbed, cooked, and quartered

2 medium zucchini, scrubbed and cut into ¼-inch slices

¼ pound fresh mushrooms, quartered

½ teaspoon salt

10 grinds fresh pepper

1. Brown the meat in oil in an 8-quart casserole over medium-high heat.

2. Add the carrots, corn, onions, parsnips, apricots, cinnamon, water, wine, and honey. Increase the heat and cook the stew until it starts to boil, then cover and simmer for 3 minutes.

3. Meanwhile, microwave the squash halves on high for about 10 minutes in a large dish covered tightly with microwaveproof plastic wrap until a knife can just pierce the cooked squash. If using an oven, place squash in a pan filled with $\frac{1}{2}$-inch water and roast until very tender, 45–60 minutes. Uncover immediately and let cool, then scoop out the flesh and cut it into large, bite-sized chunks.

4. Add the squash, cooked potatoes, zucchini, mushrooms, salt, and pepper to the stew and simmer, covered, for 25–30 minutes, or until the meat is tender.

YIELD: 6 servings
PAIRING: Grenache, Gamay Beaujolais,
fruity Zinfandel, or Pinot Noir

"Excellent wine generates enthusiasm. And whatever you do with enthusiasm is generally successful."

Philippe de Rothschild

CHAPTER 3

PASTA AND GRAINS

Grains, which are quite neutral in flavor, quickly absorb liquids and seasonings, making them a natural for cooking with different wines. Rice, couscous, and several pasta types are offered here to show the range of styles and flavors of wines and other ingredients. Although pasta and grains usually are served as side dishes, several of the recipes with shrimp or cheese are complete enough to be main courses. Grains are important in our diets and make perfect bases for saucy vegetable, seafood and meat mixtures, or just substantial sauces. They are extremely versatile and can be cooked in liquid either on a burner or in the oven.

GREEK RICE PILAF
with Olives and Feta

This pilaf is very easy to prepare. The saltiness of the feta cheese and olives, as well as the dry Greek white wine, underscore the flavors of the ingredients and bring a hint of the Mediterranean to your table. If you prefer a sweet-salty taste, use a semidry white wine as a complement.

1 cup uncooked white rice

2 tablespoons olive oil

$\frac{1}{2}$ cup diced green pepper

$\frac{1}{4}$ cup Kalamata olives, pitted and diced (do not use canned olives)

1 cup defatted chicken broth

1 cup dry Greek white wine

2–3 ounces feta cheese, crumbled

8 grinds black pepper

$\frac{1}{4}$–$\frac{1}{2}$ teaspoon salt to taste

1. Preheat oven to 350°F. Sauté rice in oil in a large skillet for about 10 minutes over low heat. Remove from heat and transfer to a 2-quart baking dish with a lid. Add the remaining ingredients to the rice, stir, and cover.

2. Bake until the liquid is absorbed, about 50 minutes. Serve immediately.

YIELD: 4–6 servings as a side dish
PAIRING: Dry white wine such as Boutari Santorini, Greece, Buena Vista Lake County Sauvignon Blanc, California, or Zonnebloom Grand Soleil, South Africa. Also semidry white wine such as Chenin Blanc or Riesling.

BAKED BROWN RICE
with Water Chestnuts

The nutty flavor and texture of brown rice make it a substantial, comforting food. This easy, baked version gets Asian accents from soy sauce and water chestnuts and an earthiness from mushrooms. This dish is an especially nice accompaniment for roast turkey, chicken, or Cornish hen. For a vegetarian version, use water or vegetable broth.

1 cup semidry white wine (such as Chenin Blanc or German semidry Riesling)

1 cup defatted, low-sodium chicken broth, water, or vegetable broth

1 tablespoon corn oil

1 tablespoon soy sauce (low-sodium can be substituted)

Several grinds freshly ground black pepper

$\frac{1}{4}$ pound fresh mushrooms, coarsely chopped

1 or 2 celery stalks, sliced

$\frac{1}{2}$ cup water chestnuts, fresh if available, coarsely chopped

$\frac{1}{4}$ cup raisins

1 cup uncooked brown rice

$\frac{1}{3}$ cup chopped nuts (walnuts, pecans, or hazelnuts)

1. Preheat oven to 350°F. In a 1$\frac{1}{2}$ quart ovenproof casserole or saucepan, combine wine, broth, oil, soy sauce, pepper, and mushrooms; stir and bring to a boil over medium-high heat.

2. Remove from heat. Add celery, water chestnuts, raisins, and rice. Stir. Sprinkle nuts on top, cover, and bake for 45 minutes.

3. Uncover and bake until liquid is absorbed and rice is tender, about 15–20 minutes. Serve immediately.

YIELD: 4 servings as a side dish
PAIRING: Chenin Blanc, German semidry Riesling, or Semillon with poultry; Grenache, Gamay Beaujolais, or Pinot Noir with red meat

VINEYARD PASTA
with White Wine Sauce

Vineyard Pasta, made with green "grape leaves" and white and purple "grape clusters," is quite festive and appropriate for a meal with wine. This pasta is sold at some specialty and winery gift shops. Since the colors fade when the pasta is cooked, add red and green bell peppers for both color and flavor accents. In this dish, dry white wine is reduced for more intense flavor. Vegetarians can substitute concentrated or reduced vegetable broth for chicken broth.

1 15-ounce package Vineyard Pasta or other sturdy,
shaped pasta (rotini spirals, bows, or wheels)
$\frac{1}{4}$ cup or slightly more olive oil
$\frac{2}{3}$ cup chopped onion
2 green onions, sliced
8 medium mushrooms, sliced
1 medium red or green bell pepper (or $\frac{1}{2}$ each),
seeded, thinly sliced
1 small zucchini, thinly sliced
1 tablespoon chopped fresh basil
or $\frac{3}{4}$ teaspoon dried basil
1 tablespoon chopped fresh oregano
or $\frac{3}{4}$ teaspoon dried oregano
$\frac{1}{3}$ cup defatted chicken broth
or concentrated vegetable broth
Salt and pepper to taste
$\frac{2}{3}$ cup dry white wine (Pinot Grigio
or Sauvignon Blanc)
$\frac{1}{3}$ cup grated Parmesan cheese

1. In a large pot, bring 1 gallon salted water to a boil. When water is boiling, cook pasta according to package directions until al dente (tender-firm). Drain and keep warm.

2. Heat the oil in a medium skillet. Add chopped and sliced onions and sauté for about 8 minutes, stirring, until the onions are translucent.

3. Add mushrooms, pepper, and zucchini to the mixture, stirring for 2 minutes.

4. Add herbs, chicken broth, salt, and pepper. Bring to a boil, reduce heat, and simmer for about 8 minutes, until the liquid has almost evaporated and the sauce has thickened.

5. In a small nonreactive saucepan, heat the wine over medium heat and simmer until it is reduced by half. Add the reduced wine to the sauce and simmer for 4 minutes, or until the liquid is reduced by a third.

6. Serve sauce over pasta, tossing to coat well. Top with Parmesan cheese. Salt and pepper to taste.

YIELD: 10 first-course servings; 5–6 main-course servings
PAIRING: Dry Italian white such as Pinot Grigio, or Sauvignon Blanc; light red wine such as Grenache or Gamay Beaujolais

JARLSBERG PASTA PRIMAVERA

For a hearty and attractive pasta dish, try this one with Norwegian Jarlsberg cheese. It's a balanced vegetarian meal in a dish, where the cheese is mixed with tomatoes, pasta, and a variety of vegetables. Fresh basil adds intense flavor, toasted pine nuts provide a bit of texture, and the cheese binds the various elements together. A dry white wine without wood aging gives a magical, fresh accent to the dish and is nice to drink with it.

1 pound short pasta, such as rotini, fusilli, or penne

2 tablespoons tightly packed minced garlic,
about 6–8 cloves

2 tablespoons olive oil

1 cup dry white wine (Chardonnay with no wood
aging or Pinot Grigio)

1¼ pounds fresh spinach, rinsed, drained, and chopped
or 2 packages (10 ounces each) frozen leaf spinach,
thawed, well drained, and chopped

1 medium zucchini, thinly sliced

1 medium yellow squash, thinly sliced

1½ ounces (about ¾ cup) loosely packed fresh basil,
chopped, or 2½ tablespoons dried basil

1–1½ pound fresh plum or Roma tomatoes, chopped
(reserve juice)

¼ teaspoon freshly ground pepper

¾ pound Jarlsberg cheese, shredded

1 cup (⅓ pound) pine nuts

1. In a large pot, bring 1 gallon salted water to a boil. When water is boiling, cook pasta according to package directions until al dente (tender-firm). Drain and keep warm.

2. Cook garlic in oil for 5 minutes in a medium saucepan over low heat.

3. Add wine, spinach, zucchini, squash, and basil; cook for 15 minutes, stirring often.

4. Add tomatoes and pepper to the spinach mixture. Stir and cook for 5 minutes. Remove from heat.

5. Add cheese and nuts to pasta. Add spinach mixture, toss well, and serve immediately.

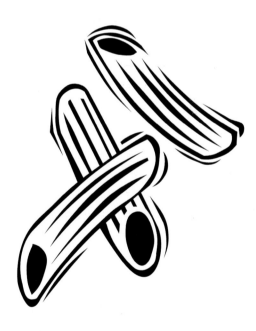

YIELD: 10–12 servings as a first course or side dish; 5–6 servings as a main dish
PAIRING: Chardonnay with no wood aging, Sauvignon Blanc, or Pinot Grigio

ROTINI WITH SHRIMP, VEGETABLES, AND RED WINE

This colorful pasta dish with green pepper, tomato, and shrimp is especially attractive when made with rotini (spiral-shaped pasta). Use fresh basil if you can get it. This pasta can be served either as an appetizer or a main course. Chianti is wonderful both as an ingredient and as a wine to serve with the dish. Round out the menu with antipasti, bread sticks, and Italian cookies for dessert.

2 tablespoons plus 1 teaspoon olive oil
12 ounces short pasta, such as rotini, fusilli, or penne
1 large onion, chopped
2 to 3 large cloves garlic, minced or pressed
1 large, green bell pepper, seeded and chopped
$\frac{3}{4}$ cup plus 2 tablespoons light, dry red wine
(such as Chianti)
$2\frac{1}{2}$ pounds fresh plum tomatoes, stem ends removed,
chopped, and drained or 1 28-ounce can Italian
tomatoes in purée
$\frac{1}{2}$ ounce ($\frac{1}{4}$ cup, loosely packed) fresh basil, chopped
1 pound medium shrimp, peeled, deveined, and
coarsely chopped
$\frac{1}{2}$ teaspoon red pepper flakes (optional)
Salt and freshly ground black pepper to taste
Grated Parmesan or Romano cheese to taste (optional)

1. In a large pot, bring 3 quarts salted water to boil. Add 1 teaspoon oil to the boiling water. Stir in the pasta and cook, following package directions, until al dente (tender-firm). Drain and keep warm.

2. Heat the remaining 2 tablespoons of oil in a medium saucepan over medium-high heat. Add onion,

garlic, and pepper; sauté until they are soft, about 10 minutes. Add the wine and simmer 2 minutes. Stir in tomatoes and basil, return the mixture to a boil and cook for an additional 10 minutes, stirring occasionally.

3. Add the shrimp and red pepper flakes to the tomato mixture. Reduce heat to medium and cook about 2 minutes, stirring, until the shrimp turn pink. Add salt and more pepper to taste.

4. Transfer pasta to a large bowl. Add the sauce and toss well. Sprinkle with grated cheese, if desired.

YIELD: 6–8 servings as first course; 4–5 servings as main course
PAIRING: Dry, light, red wine such as Frescobaldi Castello Di Nipozzano Riserve Chianti Rufina, or an Oregon or California Pinot Noir

COUSCOUS WITH WINE AND SEVEN VEGETABLES

During three trips to Morocco, I fell in love with the cuisine of this North African country and returned home with a briefcase full of great recipes. Moroccan food uses many vegetables and sweet spices, and couscous (semolina grains) is one of the staples. Moroccan couscous is served with the traditional spicy harissa sauce (which is not wine-friendly). It's omitted here because this dish is so flavorful on its own and great with wine.

2 tablespoons olive oil

3 medium onions, thinly sliced

5 garlic cloves

2 zucchini, thinly sliced

1 yellow squash, thinly sliced

$\frac{1}{2}$ small eggplant, peeled, quartered, thinly sliced, salted, and drained or 1 15-ounce can whole peeled tomatoes, drained

$1\frac{1}{2}$ cups dry white wine (Sauvignon Blanc, Pinot Blanc, or dry white varietal blend)

2 cups defatted chicken or vegetable broth

$\frac{1}{2}$ pound green beans, stem ends trimmed and sliced into 2-inch strips

2 carrots, cut into $\frac{1}{2}$-inch dice

1 sweet potato, cut into $\frac{1}{2}$-inch dice

1 16-ounce can of chick peas, drained and rinsed

$\frac{1}{2}$ cup raisins

1 teaspoon sugar

1 teaspoon cumin

$\frac{1}{2}$ teaspoon red pepper flakes to taste

$\frac{1}{2}$ teaspoon salt

1 teaspoon cinnamon

$1\frac{1}{4}$ cups water

$1\frac{1}{2}$ cups instant couscous

1. Heat oil in a large sauté pan over medium heat. Sauté onions and garlic for about 5 minutes until onions are translucent. Add zucchini, squash, and eggplant or tomatoes. Cook for 5 minutes, stirring frequently.

2. Add $\frac{1}{2}$ cup wine, broth, green beans, carrots, sweet potato, chick peas, raisins, sugar, $\frac{1}{2}$ teaspoon cumin, red pepper flakes, salt, and cinnamon. Bring to a boil, then lower heat and simmer covered for 30 minutes until carrots and sweet potatoes are tender.

3. Meanwhile, prepare the couscous. In a small pot, bring the remaining cup of wine, water, and remaining $\frac{1}{2}$ teaspoon of cumin to a boil. Lower heat, add the couscous, and stir for 2 minutes. Remove from heat, cover, and set aside.

4. Place the vegetable mixture and the couscous in separate bowls. To serve, spoon vegetable mixture over the couscous.

YIELD: 6 servings
PAIRING: Semidry white wine, such as Chenin Blanc or Riesling, or light red wine, such as Grenache or Gamay Beaujolais

RISOTTO WITH LEEKS AND FENNEL

From the great variety of risottos I have enjoyed, this is a favorite. This recipe was adapted from the Buena Vista Carneros, California's oldest premium winery. The Buena Vista Carneros Chardonnay offers just the right flavor dimension to the finished dish, balancing the tastes of leek, onion, and fennel that seem to melt into the rice.

1 medium leek
1 medium bulb fresh fennel
1 tablespoon butter
1–2 tablespoons olive oil
$\frac{1}{2}$ cup chopped sweet onion (Spanish or Walla Walla)
Salt and freshly ground black pepper
$\frac{1}{3}$ cup water
2 cups chicken broth combined with $1\frac{3}{4}$ cups water
$1\frac{1}{2}$ cups arborio rice
$\frac{2}{3}$ cup dry white wine (Buena Vista Chardonnay)
3 tablespoons minced parsley
$\frac{1}{3}$ cup freshly grated Parmesan cheese

1. Prepare the leek and fennel by halving bulbs, and removing the thick, tough outer layers. Cut each half again through the core, remove the core, rinse thoroughly, and drain. Cut the pieces crosswise into thin slices.

2. Heat $\frac{1}{2}$ tablespoon of the butter and oil in a large saucepan over moderate heat. Add the onion and sauté until it is softened, about 4 minutes.

3. Add the leek, fennel, salt, and pepper, and stir to coat with the seasonings. Add water, bring to a simmer, cover, and adjust heat to maintain a simmer. Cook for 20–25 minutes until the fennel is tender, stirring occasionally.

4. In another large saucepan, bring the broth/water mixture to a simmer. Adjust the heat to keep liquid just below boiling.

5. Add the rice to the leek and fennel mixture, stirring to blend. When the rice is hot throughout, add the wine.

6. When the wine evaporates, begin adding the hot broth $\frac{1}{2}$ cup at a time, stirring constantly and adding more broth only when the previous addition has been absorbed. Adjust heat so the mixture simmers steadily but not briskly. It should take 20–25 minutes for the rice to absorb all the broth and become tender. At that point, it should be creamy and the rice grains should have a touch of firmness at the center.

7. Cover, remove from heat, and let mixture stand for 5 minutes. Uncover and stir in the parsley, Parmesan cheese, and remaining butter. Serve in warm bowls for a first course or as a side dish.

YIELD: 4–6 servings
PAIRING: Buena Vista Carneros Estate Chardonnay or Sauvignon Blanc

"If wine interferes
with your business,
put your business aside."

Spanish Proverb

CHAPTER 4
POULTRY
AND MEAT DISHES

P oultry and meat are the backbone of many of our menus, and they can be prepared to be wine-friendly. For these recipes, wine is a key ingredient. It plays several roles, including adding flavor and liquid to a dish, tenderizing meat when used as a marinade, and deglazing the pans. The recipes in this chapter use various cooking methods, from sautéing and braising on the burner to roasting, broiling, and grilling.

BRATWURSTS
in Mustard-White Wine Sauce

These bratwursts are especially good with mixed grilled vegetables, such as bell peppers and onions, and served over egg noodles. Pour a German wine for both tradition and good, compatible taste.

4 cooked bratwursts (or French boudin blanc
sausages), slashed in 3 or 4 places
3 tablespoons butter
3 medium cloves garlic, coarsely chopped
1⅓ cups dry, fruity white wine (such as Riesling or
Chenin Blanc)
1 tablespoon Dijon mustard
2–3 tablespoons minced green onion
2 teaspoons minced fresh dill
Salt and freshly ground black pepper

1. Grill sausages over medium-hot coals or broil in a broiler about 5 inches from the heat, turning to lightly brown all sides, 5–6 minutes. Transfer cooked sausages to a warm serving platter; keep warm.

2. In a small saucepan, melt butter. Add garlic and sauté until golden. Remove garlic with a slotted spoon and set aside.

3. Increase heat to medium-high; cook butter until foamy and light brown. Quickly stir in wine; cook and stir until reduced by half. Add Dijon mustard, then whisk until mixture is smooth, another 1–2 minutes. Add green onion, dill, salt, pepper, and reserved garlic. Pour sauce over sausages and serve.

YIELD: 4 servings
PAIRING: Riesling, Chenin Blanc, or Semillon

GRILLED MARINATED RIB STEAKS

The Benziger Family Winery, Glen Ellen, California, created this delicious recipe to showcase their Estate Tribute Red, one of two estate wines named to pay tribute to the family's late patriarch, Bruno Benziger.

6 12-ounce rib steaks
½ cup light olive oil
½ cup red wine vinegar
½ cup red wine (Benziger Estate Tribute Red or a
smooth Cabernet Sauvignon)
3 cloves garlic, minced
1 tablespoon chopped fresh rosemary
1 tablespoon chopped fresh thyme
1 tablespoon chopped fresh oregano
1 teaspoon salt
2 teaspoons pepper
3 tablespoons soy sauce
1 tablespoon brown sugar
Pinch of red pepper

1. Rinse steaks and pat dry. Arrange steaks in a shallow glass or nonmetallic pan.

2. Place remaining ingredients in a blender container; blend thoroughly. Pour marinade over steaks, turning them to coat both sides. Cover and refrigerate for 2–6 hours.

3. Remove steaks from the refrigerator ½ hour before grilling; drain off the marinade. Grill steaks over medium-hot coals until medium-rare, about 5–6 minutes per side.

Yield: 6 servings
Pairing: Benziger Estate Tribute Red

WHITE MERLOT-MARINATED CHICKEN BREASTS

I created this succulent grilled chicken recipe especially to use with a lovely pink-tinted white Merlot from France. Chicken is marinated in a basil, garlic, and wine mixture, then broiled to crisp, golden perfection. Round out your menu with broiled potato halves and zucchini slices, followed by a fresh fruit plate with sorbet or sugar cookies for dessert. Pour Chenin Blanc into glasses to toast a great dinner.

2 large skinless chicken breasts, quartered and trimmed of excess fat

1 cup white Merlot, or similiar blush or rosé wine

$\frac{1}{4}$ cup extra virgin olive oil

2 tablespoons fresh lemon juice

1 medium clove garlic, crushed

1 tablespoon chopped fresh basil

or 1 teaspoon crushed dried basil

2 tablespoons chopped fresh parsley

2 teaspoons minced fresh chives

Salt and freshly ground black pepper

1. Rinse chicken and pat dry with paper towels. Place in a shallow glass dish.

2. In a small bowl or large measuring cup, mix the wine with olive oil, lemon juice, garlic, basil, parsley, and chives. Pour marinade over chicken, turning the meat to soak all sides. Marinate for at least 30 minutes.

3. Preheat the broiler. Remove chicken from marinade, place in broiler pan, and broil five inches from heat for 10–12 minutes per side, turning once, and basting with the marinade until it is all used. Do not use any leftover, uncooked marinade. A meat thermometer inserted into the chicken breast, away from fat or bone, should register 185°F when it is done. Remove chicken from the broiler, season with salt and pepper, and serve.

YIELD: 4 servings
PAIRING: Chenin Blanc or the French white Merlot (or another dry rosé wine) used in the dish. Grenache is another good choice.

SAUTÉED STEAKS
with Pinot Noir Butter and Toasted Rosemary

Boneless rib steaks are quickly prepared in a skillet and a Pinot Noir is used for deglazing the pan. Venison steaks are also great as a substitute. Toasted rosemary sprigs add a final flavorful touch.

4 boneless steaks from the rib section
(Delmonico or club) about 8 ounces each,
cut 1-inch thick and trimmed
$\frac{1}{4}$ cup canola or olive oil
Salt and freshly ground pepper to taste
$\frac{3}{4}$ cup Pinot Noir
2 tablespoons softened butter
4 sprigs rosemary
Garnish: curly endive

1. Trim excess fat from steaks; slash their edges in several places to prevent them from curling during cooking. Rinse and pat dry.

2. In a large, heavy skillet, heat 2 tablespoons oil over medium-high heat.

3. Brown steaks on both sides; sauté until they reach desired doneness, turning once (for rare steaks, this will take about 3 minutes per side). Remove steaks from heat and transfer to warmed serving plates. Season with salt and pepper; keep warm.

4. Remove the excess fat from the pan and add the wine. Increase the heat to high and stir to loosen drippings. Cook, stirring, until the mixture is reduced to $\frac{1}{3}$ cup and has the consistency of a thin syrup. Remove it from the heat and gradually stir in softened butter; the butter sauce should be a creamy consistency.

5. In a small skillet, heat the remaining oil. Brown rosemary for $1\frac{1}{2}$ minutes, turning to cook all sides.

6. To serve, pour sauce around each steak. Top with toasted rosemary, and garnish with curly endive.

YIELD: 4 servings
PAIRING: A rich, flavorful Pinot Noir, such as Gloria Ferrar 1994 Carneros Pinot Noir, also, Petite Sirah or Cabernet Sauvignon

DR. FRANK'S CHICKEN
with Gewürztraminer

The late Dr. Konstantin Frank, New York State's legendary winemaker, pioneered the growing of the esteemed European vinifera grapes in the Northeast. His Vinifera Wine Cellars, now run by his son, Willy Frank, is above Keuka Lake in the beautiful Finger Lakes region. I've had the pleasure of being a guest there and enjoying a dinner that included a selection of Willy's fine, award-winning wines. Willy's family makes a grilled rabbit with Gewürztraminer, and I've adapted their recipe to chicken and the broiler.

2½–3 pounds broiler-fryer chicken, cut up and skinned
(Leave the skin on during cooking for a more moist
chicken, but remove when eating to avoid the fat.)
1 cup Gewürztraminer
⅓ cup olive oil
½ cup cider vinegar
4 large cloves garlic, minced
Grated peel of 1 lime
Juice of 1 lime (1 tablespoon)
1 bunch cilantro, minced, to taste

1. Rinse chicken, pat dry with paper towels, and place in a large glass dish or bowl. Set aside.

2. In a small bowl, mix wine, oil, vinegar, garlic, lime peel and juice, and cilantro. Pour mixture over chicken. Cover chicken and refrigerate for at least 4 hours.

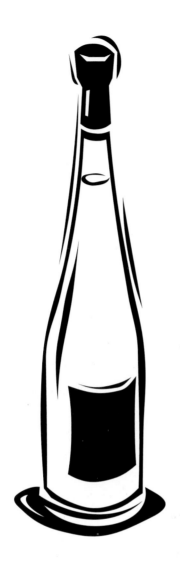

3. Preheat the broiler. Drain off the marinade and discard. Broil the chicken, exterior side down for 20–25 minutes. (Breasts will cook faster than legs.) Turn the chicken over, basting with juice from the broiler pan. Broil the chicken until juices run clear when pierced with a paring knife.

YIELD: 4 servings
PAIRING: A semidry Gewürztraminer such as
Dr. Konstantin Frank, or dry Johannisberg Riesling

STEAK WITH MUSHROOM-MERLOT SAUCE

A London broil is a flavorful meat cut that takes well to marinating and can be broiled in minutes. A full-bodied Merlot with plum and herb flavors is used for the marinade and, when enriched with mushrooms, herbs, and a bit of cream, makes a delightful sauce. Accompany the London broil with wide egg noodles and steamed carrots. Pour a Merlot or a Cabernet Sauvignon with characteristic plum or black currant tastes to enjoy with the meal.

1 cup Merlot

2 tablespoons olive oil

1 tablespoon fresh thyme or 1 teaspoon dried thyme

2–2$\frac{1}{2}$ pounds London broil (or a "family" steak)

3 shallots, minced

3–5 cloves garlic, crushed

8 ounces mushrooms, thinly sliced

$\frac{1}{3}$ cup whipping cream

$\frac{1}{4}$ teaspoon salt

8 grinds black pepper

2 tablespoons tomato paste

1. Make marinade by mixing wine, 1 tablespoon of oil, and thyme in a 2-cup glass measure or small bowl.

2. Rinse steak and pat dry, then place in shallow glass dish. Pour marinade over the steak and turn the meat to coat both sides. Cover and refrigerate at least 2 hours or up to overnight, turning once or twice.

3. Remove steak from the marinade. In a heavy, medium-sized saucepan, heat the remaining tablespoon of oil. Sauté shallots and garlic for 3 minutes over

low heat, stirring. Pour in the wine marinade and bring it to a boil; let it boil until it is slightly reduced, about 10 minutes. Add the mushrooms, then lower the heat and cook them until soft, about 5 minutes. Add cream, salt, pepper, and tomato paste; simmer for 3 minutes.

4. Preheat the broiler. Broil steak 3 inches from heat, about 4 minutes per side for medium-rare.

5. Slice the steak thinly on the diagonal (against the grain); arrange on a platter, cover with the sauce, and serve immediately.

YIELD: 6 servings
PAIRING: Buena Vista Carneros Merlot, Cinnabar Cabernet Sauvignon from California's Central Coast, or the Australian Wyndham Estate BIN 444 Cabernet Sauvignon

HAM AND POTATO GRATIN

I've tasted similar gratins in France made with a crisp French white wine and Gruyère cheese. This version uses Riesling and the flavorful Danish Havarti caraway cheese. Leftover ham can be substituted for prosciutto.

2 tablespoons butter

3 tablespoons flour

1 cup milk

1 teaspoon Dijon mustard

Several grinds black pepper

$\frac{1}{2}$ teaspoon salt

1 bay leaf

1 tablespoon minced fresh sage

$\frac{1}{2}$ cup semidry Riesling

3 drops Tabasco or other hot sauce

2 pounds small potatoes, cooked and sliced

2 large onions, sliced, sautéed 10 minutes
in 2 tablespoons oil

$\frac{1}{4}$ pound prosciutto, diced

1 10-ounce box frozen peas

4–6 ounces Havarti cheese, shredded

1. Make a white sauce by melting butter in a small saucepan over low heat. Add flour and cook, stirring 5 minutes until incorporated and thickened. Add milk slowly, whisking thoroughly to prevent lumps. When smooth and thick, add mustard, black pepper, salt, bay leaf, sage, wine, and Tabasco. Cook over low heat 1 minute. Discard bay leaf and set sauce aside.

2. Preheat oven to 375° F. In a baking pan with low sides (a 9-inch cake pan works nicely), layer sauce, potatoes, onions, prosciutto, and peas, sprinkling cheese on each layer. Start and end with sauce.

3. Bake uncovered about 40 minutes, until bubbly and golden-brown. Serve hot as a main course.

YIELD: 4–6 main-course servings
PAIRING: Dry Riesling, Pinot Blanc, or Sauvignon Blanc

DUCK BREASTS
with Blackberry Sauce

Fruity red wine and blackberry jam join forces for this sensuous sauce that flavors boneless duck breasts. This makes a luscious entrée or first course that is simple to prepare.

4 6-ounce boneless duck breasts
Salt and freshly ground black pepper

BLACKBERRY RED WINE SAUCE

1½ tablespoons butter
1 tablespoon honey
⅔ cup defatted chicken stock
½ cup fruity, medium-bodied red wine such as Merlot,
Zinfandel, Pinot Noir, or Chianti
1 small shallot, minced
¼ cup seedless blackberry jam
1 tablespoon minced fresh thyme or marjoram
or ¾ teaspoon dried
Salt and freshly ground black pepper

1. Preheat oven to 375° F. Rinse duck and pat dry, then season duck breasts with a little salt and pepper. In nonstick skillet, sear skin-side down until browned. Pour off excess duck fat and reserve in refrigerator for another use.

2. Transfer duck breasts skin-side-up onto roasting pan. Roast in oven 15 minutes, or until meat tests done. (Juices should run clear when pierced with a paring knife.) While duck is roasting, prepare the sauce.

3. To make sauce, melt butter in small saucepan over low heat. Stir in honey. Cook, whisking, until blended.

4. Whisk in stock, wine, and shallot. Increase heat and bring to a boil. Add jam and season with thyme or marjoram, salt, and pepper. Reduce heat and simmer, stirring occasionally, about 15 minutes.

5. Taste and adjust seasonings. Increase heat, bring to a low boil and reduce sauce until it starts to thicken and will lightly coat a spoon. Keep warm until ready to serve.

6. When duck is done, remove from oven. Meat thermometer should register 180°F. Let stand several minutes. Remove fatty skin and transfer to serving plates. Spoon sauce over duck.

YIELD: 2 servings as an entrée; 4 servings as a first course
PAIRING: Medium-bodied Merlot, Zinfandel, Pinot Noir, or Chianti

STIRRED-CRAZY STEAK AND VEGETABLES

Stir-fried foods are especially popular now because of their flexibility and healthfulness. You can make this stir-fry dish using a wok or a large skillet and a wok utensil for tossing. Any vegetable except the scallion may be eliminated without affecting the results. Garlic is essential here, and the Cabernet Sauvignon adds a distinctive rich taste to the sauce. If you prefer another dry red wine, select a Zinfandel, a Merlot, or perhaps one of the wonderful Italian reds.

2 tablespoons corn, canola, or peanut oil

1 pound flank steak, thinly sliced across the grain

3 medium carrots, cut into 2 x $\frac{1}{4}$-inch strips

2 small parsnips, cut into 2 x $\frac{1}{4}$-inch strips

8 ounces Asian rice noodles (or linguine)

1 bunch scallions, sliced

4 cloves garlic, minced

1 red bell pepper, seeded and coarsely chopped

1 green bell pepper, seeded and coarsely chopped

2 cups loosely packed, coarsely chopped spinach

Wine Sauce (see recipe at right)

1. In a wok or a large, heavy skillet, heat 2 teaspoons of oil over medium-high heat. Rinse steak and pat dry, then quickly stir-fry until it is barely cooked. Remove from the pan.

2. Heat 2 more teaspoons oil; add carrots and parsnips. Stir-fry, tossing constantly, over medium-high heat for 5 minutes. Remove cooked vegetables from the pan.

3. Meanwhile, cook noodles in a large pot of salted boiling water, following the package directions. Drain and cover.

4. Prepare the Wine Sauce (see recipe below).

5. Add remaining 2 teaspoons oil, scallions, garlic, and red and green pepper to wok. Stir-fry, tossing constantly, over medium-high heat for 5 minutes. Add the spinach and cook for an additional minute.

6. Stir in the Wine Sauce, beef, carrots, and turnips. Bring the mixture to a boil, reduce heat, and simmer just until the sauce thickens, about 1 minute. Add noodles to the wok, stirring to heat. Serve immediately.

WINE SAUCE

2 teaspoons cornstarch
$\frac{1}{2}$–$\frac{3}{4}$ cup Cabernet Sauvignon
1 tablespoon honey
2 tablespoons soy sauce, or to taste (low-sodium can be substituted)
2 tablespoons bottled barbecue sauce (not smoky type)
$\frac{1}{4}$ teaspoon crushed red pepper flakes
1 teaspoon Worcestershire sauce

1. In a small bowl, combine cornstarch with wine, stirring until dissolved.

2. Stir in honey, soy sauce, barbecue sauce, red pepper flakes, and Worcestershire sauce. Set aside until ready to cook (see step 6 above).

YIELD: 4 servings
PAIRING: Cabernet Sauvignon, Merlot, or Barbera

SAGE-ROASTED ROCK CORNISH GAME HENS

Cornish game hens make an attractive presentation for a special dinner. Here, they are roasted with a butter-oil baste at a high temperature to start the browning; then they get a flavorful wine bath with lots of sage. Serve with rice, a green vegetable, steamed carrots, and more of the Chenin Blanc.

4 Rock Cornish game hens, 20–22 ounces each

Salt and freshly ground pepper

3 stalks celery, halved lengthwise

1 medium onion, cut into 5 slices

$\frac{1}{4}$ cup melted butter

2 tablespoons canola oil

1 teaspoon chopped fresh sage or $\frac{1}{4}$ teaspoon dried

MARINADE

$\frac{2}{3}$ cup Chenin Blanc

$\frac{1}{2}$ cup chicken broth

1 sweet onion, sliced $\frac{1}{2}$-inch thick

1 tablespoon chopped fresh sage or 1 teaspoon dried

1. Preheat the oven to 425°F. Rinse hens; remove giblets, rinse hen cavities, and lightly add salt and pepper.

2. Place giblets, 1 stalk celery, and 1 slice onion in a medium saucepan. Add lightly salted water to cover and simmer, covered, for about 45 minutes over low heat until the giblets are tender.

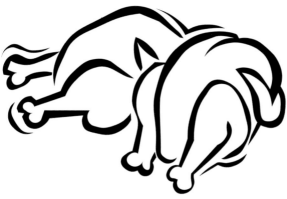

3. Remove giblets with a slotted spoon and chop finely; then set aside. Reserve broth and giblets for sauce.

4. Combine melted butter, oil, and 1 teaspoon of sage in a glass measuring cup. Set aside. Make the marinade by combining the wine, broth, sweet onion, and sage.

5. Place half a stalk of celery and one of the remaining onion slices into each hen. Truss the hens with small skewers or large wooden picks; tie the legs together with string for a nicer presentation. Arrange hens in a shallow roasting pan, breast side up. Brush butter-oil mixture over them. Sprinkle lightly with salt and pepper if desired. Roast for 20 minutes.

6. Spoon marinade over hens. Reduce oven temperature to 350°F and roast for about 35 minutes more, basting frequently with pan sauce until the meat is tender and browned.

7. Transfer hens to warmed platter; keep warm. For sauce, skim the excess fat from pan juices. Stir $\frac{1}{2}$ cup of giblet broth into the pan, scraping to loosen brown bits while bringing the liquid to a boil. Add sweet onion slices from marinade and adjust the seasonings. Cover and simmer for 2–3 minutes until the onions are softened. Add giblets; heat until warm. Serve sauce with the hens.

YIELD: 4 servings
PAIRING: Chenin Blanc, Riesling, or Semillon

ROAST RACK OF LAMB PROVENÇAL

Cabernet Sauvignon is the classic match with roast lamb. This dish is redolent of herbs and Dijon mustard and uses wine to deglaze the pan. It is a perfect, elegant main course for a dinner party accompanied by new potatoes and asparagus (see Appendix A, p. 131).

2 racks of lamb with bones frenched,
about 2 pounds each
1 large clove garlic, crushed
1½ teaspoons crushed Provençal herbs (rosemary,
thyme, basil, marjoram, savory; this blend
is available premixed)
Freshly ground black pepper
About 1 teaspoon olive oil
Salt
½–¾ cup defatted pan juices (from cooking the lamb)
or stock (beef stock may be substituted)
½ cup dry red wine, such as Cabernet Sauvignon
1 teaspoon Dijon mustard
1 teaspoon (or slightly more) butter
Pinch of crushed Provençal herbs
Garnish: preserved kumquats and watercress

1. Before you begin cooking, rinse lamb and pat dry. Let stand at room temperature for 20 minutes. Preheat the oven to 450°F.

2. In a small bowl, mix crushed garlic, herbs, pepper, and oil. Rub the lamb well with this mixture.

3. Place meat, fat-side up, on a rack in an open roasting pan. Roast in the oven for about 20 minutes, until it is browned but still pink inside. An instant-read meat thermometer inserted away from the bone and fat should register 145°F or 155°F, depending on

your preference for medium-rare or medium doneness. The temperature will continue to rise after lamb is removed from oven until it reaches 150°F for medium-rare or 160°F for medium. Remove lamb from the oven and place it on a board or hot platter. Cover and let it stand for several minutes.

4. Meanwhile, remove most of the fat from pan juices. This method of cooking does not yield many pan juices, so add stock to measure $\frac{1}{2}$ cup. Deglaze the pan with wine, scraping up any baked-on drippings. Transfer contents of pan to a saucepan.

5. Over medium heat, whisk in mustard, butter, and a pinch of the herbs. Keep hot until ready to serve.

6. To serve, carve rack into chops. Decorate bones with paper frills and arrange 2–3 chops over a serving of sauce on each plate. Garnish with kumquats and watercress. Add salt to taste. Surround chops with tiny new potatoes in their jackets and asparagus with lemon butter.

YIELD: 4 servings
PAIRING: Cabernet Sauvignon, from California or France

CHICKEN AND LEMON DUMPLINGS

This unusual recipe by Beringer Vineyards' Executive Chef Jerry Comfort was developed for "Wines of the Pacific Rim," a Hong Kong conference where Comfort was a guest chef. He says this chicken may be prepared a day in advance of serving—a real convenience when entertaining. Prepare the dumplings just before cooking, then top the chicken with the dumpling batter and bake. This is double comfort food!

4 whole chicken legs (boneless chicken breasts
may be substituted)
Salt and freshly ground black pepper
2 tablespoons olive oil
4–6 leeks, rinsed and cut into $\frac{1}{4}$-inch rings (use white
part up to the light green)
1 white onion, thinly sliced
1 cup Beringer Chardonnay
2 cups defatted concentrated chicken stock
1 sprig tarragon plus 1 teaspoon chopped fresh
tarragon leaves or $\frac{1}{2}$ teaspoon dried tarragon
$\frac{1}{2}$ cup cream (half-and-half or whipping)
8 ounces oyster mushrooms, trimmed and brushed
(porcini or shiitake mushrooms may be used)
8 ounces pearl onions, roasted
Lemon Dumplings (see recipe at right)

1. Preheat oven to 325°F. Rinse chicken and pat it dry; then season with salt and pepper.

2. Cook the chicken in oil in a skillet over medium heat, browning it lightly on both sides. Remove from the pan, keeping the liquid in the pan. To the same pan, add leeks and white onion; cover and sweat over medium heat until they are translucent but not browned. Add wine and cook uncovered until reduced to 2 tablespoons. Set aside.

3. In a medium ovenproof sauté pan, add chicken, chicken stock, and a sprig of tarragon. Cover and oven-braise for 45 minutes, or until meat is very tender. Remove chicken from the pan and skim fat off the stock. Reserve. Remove bones from the legs when cooled and comfortable to touch.

4. Combine leek mixture and stock in a blender or food processor bowl and purée until it is smooth. Strain over a medium bowl. Gently stir cream into sauce. At this point, the chicken and sauce may be covered and stored separately in the refrigerator overnight.

5. Prepare the Lemon Dumplings. Preheat oven to 400°F. Place the chicken in a casserole dish, add sauce (if chicken and sauce are stored overnight, reheat before using), chopped tarragon, mushrooms, and roasted pearl onions. Place large spoonfuls of dumpling batter 1 inch apart on top of the casserole contents. Bake for 15–20 minutes, until browned.

LEMON DUMPLINGS

$\frac{1}{2}$ teaspoon sugar

2 teaspoons baking powder

$\frac{1}{2}$ teaspoon salt

$1\frac{1}{2}$ cups all-purpose flour

1 egg

$\frac{1}{3}$ cup melted butter

$\frac{1}{2}$ cup buttermilk (or 1 teaspoon lemon juice stirred into $\frac{1}{2}$ cup milk and allowed to stand 5 minutes)

Zest of 1 lemon, grated

1. Sift the sugar, baking powder, salt, and flour into a medium bowl and make a well in the center.

2. In a separate bowl, mix the egg, melted butter, and buttermilk. Add the lemon zest and pour mixture into the well of dry ingredients. Stir gently until the dry ingredients are just moistened.

YIELD: 4 servings
PAIRING: Beringer Chardonnay

"A glass of wine is a great refreshment after a hard day's work."

Ludwig van Beethoven

CHAPTER 5
SEAFOOD

We are fortunate to have an abundance of fresh seafood available to us today, in part because of better transportation and quick distribution. You need not live on a coast to enjoy fresh catches from the ocean. I favor seafood and eat it often, and so I have created a large repertoire of recipes. The ones in this chapter are embellished with wine in different ways including glazing, marinating, and saucing.

Since fish and seafood are tender when they come out of the water, a marinade doesn't tenderize them. Instead, it infuses flavor and "cooks" the fish, as in ceviche (see Sauvignon Blanc Ceviche, p. 15), by making the flesh opaque. In Scallops au Naturel (p. 82), the barely cooked mollusks get a wine bath and marinate in the refrigerator, which further "cooks" them. If the suggested seafood for a recipe is not available in your area, ask your retailer to recommend appropriate substitutes. The results will still be healthful and delicious.

SALMON FILLET
with Wine-Balsamic Glaze

This preparation for salmon is one of my favorites and is very simple and quick. This dish can be prepared in a skillet as well.

2 8-ounce salmon fillets
$\frac{1}{3}$ cup Pinot Noir
2 tablespoons balsamic vinegar
1 tablespoon minced fresh dill, optional
1 medium Spanish onion, peeled, sliced $\frac{1}{4}$-inch thick
Salt and freshly ground black pepper to taste

1. Wash and trim salmon fillets so the pieces are of even thickness for broiling. Place them in a shallow glass dish. Combine wine, vinegar, and dill in a glass measuring cup. Pour over salmon. Add the onion slices, turning to moisten. Marinate for 15 minutes.

2. Preheat the broiler. Drain salmon and onions, reserve the marinade, and arrange on a broiler pan.

3. Broil salmon several inches from the heat, basting with the remaining marinade. Broil 5 minutes per side per inch of thickness. Broil thinner pieces until flesh begins to flake, about 2 minutes per side. Broil onions until they are lightly browned, about 2 minutes per side. Remove and keep warm.

4. Season with salt and pepper and serve with onions.

YIELD: 4 servings
PAIRING: Pinot Noir or Chardonnay

SEARED MEDITERRANEAN MUSSELS

The "Living Well" program developed by St. Supéry Vineyards and Winery in Napa Valley, California is based on the premise that "you are what you eat," and that healthful and delicious dining with fine wine is vital to living well. The following mussel recipe was inspired by a first course I enjoyed at a "Living Well" dinner at Shaw's Crab House in Chicago. The diced tomato garnish is called concassée.

16 mussels, cleaned, and beards
(if any) removed
1 large clove garlic, sliced
$\frac{2}{3}$ cup Chardonnay
$\frac{3}{4}$ cup diced, peeled, and seeded tomatoes
$\frac{1}{3}$ cup finely chopped fresh chervil, or 2 tablespoons
dried chervil
$\frac{1}{4}$ cup finely chopped Italian parsley

1. Heat a large pan over high heat. Add mussels to the pan and sauté for several minutes until they begin to release their liquid.

2. Add garlic and Chardonnay; cover and allow the mussels to cook until they are completely open, 4–5 minutes.

3. Add tomatoes and cook for 2–3 minutes. Add herbs, tossing lightly.

4. To serve, place four mussels in the center of each serving plate. Spoon tomato concassée on top.

YIELD: 4 servings as a first course
PAIRING: St. Supéry Chardonnay

SWORDFISH MARINATED WITH CHARDONNAY AND TARRAGON

Swordfish steaks are firm and take well to grilling and broiling. The wine marinade infuses them with flavor and makes them succulent.

4 6-ounce swordfish steaks, $\frac{1}{2}$-inch thick, rinsed and
patted dry
$\frac{2}{3}$ cup Chardonnay or Sauvignon Blanc
2 tablespoons fresh lemon juice
$\frac{1}{4}$ cup olive oil
3 medium cloves garlic, crushed
1 tablespoon plus 1 teaspoon chopped fresh tarragon
or 1 rounded teaspoon dried tarragon
2 tablespoons chopped fresh parsley
Salt and pepper
Garnish: lemon wedges

1. Place fish in a shallow glass dish. In a glass measuring cup, combine wine, lemon juice, oil, garlic, tarragon, and parsley. Pour marinade over fish, turning it to coat both sides. Marinate for 15 minutes.

2. Preheat broiler or grill. Transfer fish to broiler pan or grill rack. Broil several inches from the heat for about 4–5 minutes, then turn them over and cook 2 minutes more, occasionally basting with mari-

nade. Or grill over medium-hot coals, 3 minutes per side, following the grill manufacturer's directions. (Rule of thumb: Allow 10 minutes per inch of thickness.) Fish is done when it begins to flake when poked with a fork.

3. Remove swordfish from the heat. Add salt and pepper to taste and serve with lemon wedges.

YIELD: 4 servings
PAIRING: Wyndham Estate, Bin 222, S.E. Australian Chardonnay (full-flavored, dry, well-balanced; good Chardonnay grape taste and finish)

SPONTANEOUS TILAPIA SAUTÉ
with Chenin Blanc

For that spontaneous moment when you have a yen for a simple fish entrée, here is a very quick and easy skillet dish. This recipe features tilapia, a delicate fish that tastes good and is inexpensive. A light- to medium-bodied Chenin Blanc with its varietal flavors of grapefruit, apples, and melon or a medium-bodied Semillon with typical apricot and lemon tastes are my favorites for this dish. The wine is combined with garlic, lime juice, and lime zest and used to deglaze the pan for the sauce. The same wine makes a pleasing accompaniment to dinner.

$1\frac{1}{4}$ pounds tilapia fillets, about $\frac{1}{2}$-inch thick
(sole or sea bass can be substituted)

2 tablespoons flour

$\frac{1}{4}$ teaspoon salt

$\frac{1}{4}$ teaspoon pepper

1 large clove garlic, minced

$\frac{2}{3}$ cup Chenin Blanc or Semillon

2 tablespoons lime juice

1 teaspoon grated lime zest

2 tablespoons olive oil

4 small green onions, chopped

Garnish: minced tomato shell (halve tomato, squeeze out pulp and juice) or minced red bell pepper

1. Rinse fish and pat dry. Combine flour, salt, and pepper in a large deep bowl. Dredge fillets in flour, patting them to remove excess.

2. Combine garlic, wine, lime juice, and grated lime. Set aside.

3. Heat oil over medium-high heat in a 12-inch skillet or sauté pan (preferably nonstick). Add fillets when oil is hot but not smoking. Cook for 3 minutes. Turn fish over and cook until fillets are opaque in the center (make a small slit with a sharp knife to check the thickest part). Transfer fillets to a warmed serving platter and cover to keep warm.

4. Over high heat, add wine mixture to the skillet, scraping up cooked bits, until it is reduced by half, 2–3 minutes. Stir in green onions and cook for 1 minute more. Pour mixture over fish. Serve with a garnish of minced tomato shell or minced red bell pepper for both color and texture.

YIELD: 3–4 servings
PAIRING: Llano Estacado Winery Texas Chenin Blanc, which has enough natural residual sugar and tropical fruit bouquet to be a counterpoint with the tartness of the dish. Also, a medium-bodied Semillon or a crisp Pinot Blanc with floral tones.

SPANISH SEAFOOD STEW

During several extended visits to Spain, where I learned as much as possible about the various regional cuisines, I grew fond of zarzuela, a peppery seafood stew that is served differently in each region of the country. This red wine seafood stew (zarzuela) is my own less peppery version of this robust stew and incorporates mussels, squid, and scrod or ling cod. The wine I've selected is Torres Gran Sangre de Toro, which is produced in Penedes, Catalonia, by the Torres family. This is a classic Mediterranean-style wine with generous aromas that suggest strawberries and plums and a note of spice from the oak aging. The soft tannins ensure easy drinkability and compatibility with seafood.

3 dozen mussels

9 small squid

2 tablespoons olive oil

1 medium Spanish onion, minced

1 can (1 pound, 12 ounces) crushed peeled tomatoes in purée

1 medium tomato, chopped

1 bay leaf

$\frac{3}{4}$ cup Spanish red wine (Torres Gran Sangre de Toro)

3 medium cloves garlic, peeled and crushed

$\frac{1}{2}$ cup chopped parsley

$\frac{1}{2}$ teaspoon dried leaf thyme

$\frac{1}{4}$ cup water

2 pounds scrod or ling cod, cut into 3-inch pieces

Ground white pepper

1. Clean mussels by scraping their shells and removing beards, if any. To open them, shake in a large pan over medium heat, or cover and steam until they open. Strain and set aside the mussel liquor. Discard any unopened mussels.

2. Clean squid by cutting off the heads below the eyes. When you pull the heads off, the innards will come with them. Remove cartilage, rinse thoroughly, and dry. Slice into rings.

3. In a large skillet or pot, heat oil over medium heat. Add onion and reduce heat to medium-low. Sauté onion slowly until it is brown. Add tomatoes and bay leaf; stir. Increase the heat and cook for about 3 minutes more. Add wine, about $\frac{3}{4}$ cup of the mussel liquor, and squid rings. Bring the pot to a boil, reduce the heat, cover, and simmer for about 15 minutes.

4. In a blender or food processor, purée garlic, parsley, and thyme with water. Add the mixture to the sauce, stirring well. Bring it to a boil, reduce the heat, and simmer for about 3 minutes, until the sauce is thickened.

5. Add the mussels and fish. Cover the pot and simmer for about 10 minutes, until fish flakes. Serve in bowls; sprinkle with pepper to taste.

YIELD: 6 servings
PAIRING: Torres Gran Sangre de Toro Reserva

SCALLOPS AU NATUREL

Scallops are among my favorite shellfish, and this recipe is elegant yet simple. The scallops are barely cooked, then get a flavorful bath of a wine-vegetable-herb broth and marinate in the refrigerator until served with a wonderful curried mayonnaise. Champagne cuts the richness of the sauce and is my first choice with this.

3 cups water

1 cup dry white wine (Semillon or Chenin Blanc)

$\frac{1}{2}$ small onion, cut in half

$\frac{1}{2}$ carrot, peeled and thinly sliced

$\frac{1}{2}$ stalk celery

1 sprig parsley

$\frac{3}{4}$ teaspoon dried thyme

3 white peppercorns

$\frac{1}{2}$ teaspoon salt

1–1$\frac{1}{2}$ pounds sea scallops

Curried Mayonnaise (see recipe at right)

Garnish: dill sprigs

1. Combine water, wine, onion, carrot, celery, parsley, thyme, peppercorns, and salt in a large saucepan. Simmer over medium heat for 15 minutes. Remove pan from the heat. Strain ingredients into a large bowl, discarding any solids. Return the liquid to the saucepan.

2. Rinse scallops with cold running water; then add them to the saucepan. Barely simmer scallops uncovered over medium-low heat for about 2–3 minutes until opaque. Remove scallops with a slotted spoon and place in a medium-size bowl.

3. Remove the pan from the heat and let the liquid cool for 10 minutes, then pour it over scallops. Cover the dish and refrigerate until it is cold, about 2 hours.

4. Make Curried Mayonnaise.

5. To serve, drain scallops and serve with Curried Mayonnaise. Garnish with dill sprigs.

YIELD: 4 servings

CURRIED MAYONNAISE

2 egg yolks, at room temperature
1 egg, at room temperature
$\frac{1}{4}$ teaspoon salt
$\frac{1}{8}$ teaspoon curry powder
A few grinds of freshly ground white pepper
2 tablespoons fresh lime juice
1–1$\frac{1}{4}$ cups safflower oil

1. Combine egg yolks, egg, salt, curry powder, and pepper in a blender or food processor. Blend for 15 seconds on medium-low speed.

2. With machine running slowly, pour in lime juice and blend for 10 seconds. With the machine still running, slowly add oil in a thin, steady stream until the mixture thickens.

3. Cover and refrigerate until cold. Mayonnaise can be stored in a covered glass jar in the refrigerator for up to 3 days.

YIELD: 1$\frac{1}{3}$ cups
PAIRING: Dry sparkling wine, such as Domaine Carneros Brut or Roederer Estate Anderson Valley Brut from California; Dr. Frank, Chateau Frank Brut from New York; Domaine Ste. Michelle Blanc de Blancs from Columbia Valley, Washington. Table white wines such as Chenin Blanc or Semillon also match well.

STEAMED HALIBUT
in Savoy Cabbage

This healthful, creative halibut recipe is from Phillip Breitweiser, chef of The Café at Sonoma Mission Inn & Spa. When halibut isn't available, substitute sole, flounder, or salmon. I've doubled Phillip's original recipe, and it may be doubled again to serve four. The larger, outer leaves of the savoy cabbage are used to wrap the vegetables and fish fillet completely, so they are steamed in their own juices with a little fish stock and Sauvignon Blanc. The flavor and aroma are wonderful and should quickly convert anyone who has yet to sample the health-conscious, taste-tempting delicacies of spa food.

6 outer leaves of savoy or Napa Chinese cabbage
(available at most grocery stores)
$\frac{1}{4}$ cup julienne strips of peeled or scraped carrots
$\frac{1}{4}$ cup julienne strips of zucchini
$\frac{1}{4}$ cup julienne strips of red bell pepper
$\frac{1}{4}$ cup julienne slices of red Bermuda onion
6 sprigs tarragon
2 5–6 ounce halibut fillets, rinsed
2 lemons, sliced
2 tablespoons Sauvignon Blanc (Matanzas Creek,
Viansa, or Kenwood)
2 tablespoons fish stock or clam juice
Salt and pepper to taste

1. Blanch the cabbage leaves for about 1 minute in a pot of boiling water. Then plunge them into a cold-water bath, pat dry, and cut out the core of each cabbage leaf.

2. Place half the carrot, zucchini, bell pepper, and onion, plus two tarragon sprigs, in the bottom middle part of each of two cabbage leaves. For each portion, place one fish fillet piece on top of the vegetables and top with three lemon slices and another tarragon sprig.

3. Sprinkle half the white wine, fish stock, salt, and pepper over each unwrapped packet. For each portion, wrap a bottom leaf around the top of the fish, making sure the entire fish is wrapped tightly (you may need to cut the leaves or overwrap with a third leaf). Put the fish packets in the steamer seam-side down. Steam in a steamer or perforated pan for 12–15 minutes over simmering water or over a mixture of half water and wine. Serve hot.

YIELD: 2 servings

PAIRING: Matanzas Creek Sauvignon Blanc is Chef Phillip Breitweiser's special recommendation because it is on the fruitier side, has good body and a lingering finish, but doesn't overpower the delicate fish. He also likes the Viansa Sauvignon Blanc and the Kenwood Sauvignon Blanc for this dish.

BAY SCALLOPS WITH SNOW PEAS
and Dill Crème Fraîche

Tiny bay scallops are quickly sautéed with fresh snow peas, then served with a dilled crème fraîche sauce, tart with lime and based on clam juice and white wine. Select a Chardonnay not aged in oak, which would overpower the seafood flavor and tangy sauce. These flavorful mollusks make a stunning opener for a dinner party.

1 tablespoon minced shallots

1 rinsed leek, cut into $1\frac{1}{2}$ x $\frac{1}{8}$-inch strips (about 1 cup);
use both green and white parts

1 small red bell pepper, cut into 2 x $\frac{1}{8}$-inch strips
(about $\frac{1}{2}$ cup)

$\frac{1}{4}$ cup unsalted sweet butter

1 pound bay scallops, rinsed and drained

1 cup trimmed small snow peas (about $2\frac{1}{2}$ ounces)

$\frac{1}{4}$ cup clam juice

$\frac{1}{3}$ cup Chardonnay (not oak-aged) or Sauvignon Blanc

1 tablespoon fresh lime juice

1 tablespoon minced fresh dill

Freshly ground white pepper

3 tablespoons crème fraîche (found in specialty dairy
sections of some supermarkets. A thick yogurt or sour
cream may be substituted, but reduce the cooking heat
to very low to keep from separating.)

Garnish: several slivers lime peel and 4 sprigs dill

1. Sauté shallots, leek, and pepper strips in butter in a medium skillet over medium-low heat for 2–3 minutes. The vegetables should be slightly soft but not browned. Remove vegetables with a slotted spoon and set aside.

2. Increase the heat to medium. Add scallops and sauté just until they are opaque, 1–2 minutes. Remove with a slotted spoon; set aside.

3. Sauté snow peas for 30 seconds. Remove with a slotted spoon; set aside.

4. Add clam juice, wine, lime juice, and dill to the skillet. Bring to boil over medium heat. Cook until the liquid is reduced to $\frac{1}{2}$ cup, about 4 minutes. Add white pepper. Stir in crème fraîche and reduce heat to medium-low. Return vegetables and scallops to the pan, stirring until warm.

5. Serve immediately in 6-inch scallop shells. Garnish with lime peel and dill sprigs. (Filled shells can be covered with foil and kept warm in a low oven up to 30 minutes.)

YIELD: 4 servings as a first course
PAIRING: Chardonnay without or with little oak aging

"Good wine is a necessity of life for me."

Thomas Jefferson

CHAPTER 6
VEGETABLE ENTRÉES AND SIDES

Vegetables offer a vast array of flavors, from mild to strong and from bitter to sweet. When I add wine as an ingredient to a dish, I consider the vegetable's main flavor characteristic and then decide whether I want the wine to highlight or be a counterpoint to the basic taste. For instance, a strong-flavored vegetable like broccoli requires a robust wine partner, such as sherry; a lighter wine would be overpowered. The simplest of these recipes is the first, where the sweetness of the onions contrasts with herbal and nutty sherry flavors. Most of these vegetable recipes will probably be served as side dishes, so wine pairings are not appropriate. I have given a few, however, because when several of these dishes comprise a vegetarian meal, wine pairings are helpful.

OREGANO ONIONS IN WINE

Onions can be both strong and sweet, and they get sweeter after cooking. Oregano's touch of bitterness and distinctive flavor balance the onions. The wine chosen for this dish is a dry, rich-flavored Amontillado sherry, which adds full, nutty flavor that also contrasts with the onions' sweetness. A sweeter sherry would increase the recipe's overall sweetness too much, making it undesirable as a side dish.

12 small whole onions (about 1½ pounds), peeled
¼ cup Amontillado sherry (dry vermouth is also good with onions)
1 tablespoon minced fresh oregano, or 1 teaspoon dried oregano
1–2 tablespoons butter

1. Arrange peeled onions in a microwavable dish. Add sherry and oregano and dot with butter.

2. Cover tightly and cook in a microwave oven on high for 7–10 minutes, depending on whether you want crunchy or soft onions. Serve hot or at room temperature.

YIELD: 4–6 servings as a side dish
PAIRING: Depends on the main course, but in general, if served with poultry, a softer white wine such as Chenin Blanc, Semillon, Gewürztraminer, or Riesling would be best. If served with red meat, a fruity and light red wine such as Gamay Beaujolais or Grenache is good.

GREEN BEANS
in Tomato-Wine Sauce

A semidry red wine, such as Grenache or Gamay, adds a lively note to the tomato purée for green beans. Only small amounts of onion and garlic are required to round out the flavor harmony.

2 tablespoons olive oil

1 small onion, coarsely chopped

2 cloves garlic, sliced

1 pound green beans, stem ends trimmed, cut into thirds

Salt and pepper to taste

2 tablespoons tomato purée or sauce (homemade or canned)

2 tablespoons semidry red wine

1. Heat oil in a large sauté pan over medium heat. Sauté onion and garlic for about 5 minutes, until the onion is translucent. Add beans and sauté them briefly, stirring constantly. Add just enough water to cover the beans. Add salt and pepper and simmer until the beans are tender and the water is reduced.

2. Combine tomato purée and wine, then gently stir them into the green bean mixture. Heat thoroughly, stirring constantly.

3. Serve hot or warm.

YIELD: 4–6 servings as a side dish
PAIRING: Zinfandel, Pinot Noir, or Chianti, depending largely on the main course

SAUTÉED LEEKS AND ASPARAGUS

The combination of leeks and asparagus with a bit of sweet red pepper, thyme, and a dry white wine creates a complex, well-balanced, and colorful vegetable. Serve it at your next dinner party or special family meal.

3 tablespoons olive oil
2 large leeks, rinsed and coarsely chopped
1 red bell pepper, chopped
2 pounds asparagus, with the tough ends snapped off, cut into 1-inch pieces
2 tablespoons minced fresh thyme, or 2 teaspoons dried thyme
$\frac{2}{3}$ cup dry white wine (Castell 1994 Müller-Thurgau Trocken, from Germany)
3 tablespoons freshly grated Parmesan cheese
Salt and freshly grated black pepper

1. Heat oil in a large sauté pan or skillet. Add leeks and red pepper and cook them over medium heat for about 15 minutes, stirring frequently, until leeks are lightly browned.

2. Add asparagus, thyme, and wine. Cover the pan and cook over low heat for 5 minutes. Stir and cook for a few more minutes until the vegetables are done, 7–8 minutes total. Remove the pan from the heat and add Parmesan cheese; add salt and pepper to taste.

YIELD: 4 servings as a side dish
PAIRING: Depends on the main course. A Sauvignon Blanc stands up to the vegetal taste of asparagus and strength of the leeks.

BRAISED SPANISH SHERRIED BROCCOLI

Broccoli cooked with this Spanish twist is a flavorful preparation. It can become discolored by the sherry, so the trick is to coat it thoroughly with oil for protection. The half-and-half adds a touch of richness, but the flavors are equally good without it.

2 tablespoons slivered almonds
2½ tablespoons olive oil, or enough to coat broccoli
3 cloves garlic, peeled and lightly mashed
¾ pound broccoli, washed, dried, and separated into florets
¼ cup dry sherry
¼ cup defatted, low-sodium chicken broth
¼ cup half-and-half (optional)

1. Over medium-low heat, warm a dry wok or sauté pan large enough to hold the broccoli. Toast almonds for about 3 minutes. Remove from pan and set aside. In the same wok or pan, heat oil, then add garlic and cook until light brown. Remove garlic and discard. Add broccoli to the pan and toss it in oil to coat it well. Move broccoli up the sides of the wok or remove it from the sauté pan.

2. Add sherry to the pan, increase the heat to medium-high, and reduce until a scant ½ tablespoon remains. Add chicken broth and broccoli to the sherry, cover, and reduce the heat. Simmer for 6–7 minutes until broccoli is crisp-tender. Add cream and toss to coat the broccoli well. Remove from the heat; garnish with almonds and serve.

YIELD: 4 servings as a side dish
PAIRING: Depends on the main course. A medium-bodied white wine, such as Semillon or Riesling

CURRIED EGGPLANT AND SWEET POTATO

This vegetable combination may seem like an "odd couple," but I've discovered that sweet potatoes contrast nicely with eggplant's bitterness. A dry white wine without oak aging is best with the duo, to offset their bitter-sweet tastes. An oaky wine would clash with these dominant flavors, whereas a tannic red wine would stand up to the bitter eggplant, but not the sweetness of the potato.

3 tablespoons corn oil

1 pound yellow onions (3 medium onions)

1 tablespoon sugar

1 cup (8 ounces) regular or low-fat plain yogurt

$1\frac{1}{2}$ teaspoons curry powder

$\frac{1}{2}$ teaspoon salt

Several grinds black pepper

$\frac{1}{2}$ cup Chardonnay without wood aging (some from Argentina or California are good choices)

2 medium sweet potatoes (1 pound), sliced $\frac{1}{4}$-inch thick

1 medium eggplant, peeled, sliced $\frac{1}{2}$-inch thick, salted and patted dry with paper towels

1. Preheat the oven to 350°F. Grease a $1\frac{1}{2}$-quart covered casserole.

2. Heat oil in a medium sauté pan or skillet. Slice onions as thinly as possible and add them to the pan. Add sugar and sauté onions for about 20 minutes over medium heat. Stir often so they don't stick or burn; they should be very soft and lightly golden in appearance.

3. In a small bowl, combine yogurt, curry, salt, pepper, and wine. Mix well and add it to the pan of onions.

4. Layer potato and eggplant slices in the casserole dish; repeat about three times, topping each layer with a spoonful of onion mixture and ending with the onion mixture.

5. Cover the dish and bake for 1 hour. Serve immediately, spooning the remaining onion mixture over each serving.

YIELD: 4–6 servings as a side dish
PAIRING: Depends largely on the main course. Argentinean or California Chardonnay without much wood aging reinforces the wine in the dish. Some Sauvignon Blancs would also be good matches.

VEGETABLE MÉLANGE
with Sherry Essence

When tasting an Amontillado sherry one evening, I realized that its deep, nutty flavor would go well with the earthiness of mushrooms. So I went to the kitchen, got the mushrooms, some onions, shallots, a red pepper, and a zucchini. I picked some basil from one of my plants and began creating this dish. To get an intensified sherry taste, I reduced the wine with shallots, then added chicken broth and reduced it more. This can be done with any fortified wine or table wine to intensify the wine flavor.

14–16 large mushrooms, cleaned and
halved or quartered
1 medium zucchini, sliced $\frac{1}{4}$-inch thick
2 medium onions, sliced $\frac{1}{4}$-inch thick
1 medium red bell pepper, seeded,
cut into 2-inch strips
2 tablespoons sliced green onion
2 teaspoons fresh lemon juice
1 tablespoon chopped fresh basil or 1 teaspoon
dried basil
Sherry Essence (see recipe at right)
Steamed rice

1. Arrange vegetables in a large microwavable casserole or regular saucepan. Sprinkle with lemon juice and basil. Let stand for several minutes.

2. Prepare Sherry Essence. Pour Sherry Essence over the vegetables, stirring to coat them.

3. If using a microwave, cover and cook on high for 4 minutes. Let stand for 3 minutes. To cook over a burner, place saucepan over medium-high heat; bring to a simmer. Reduce heat to medium-low, cover, and cook 16–20 minutes, until vegetables are tender-crisp.

4. Serve over steamed rice.

YIELD: 4–6 servings as side dish
PAIRING: Depends on the main course; Merlot or Zinfandel

SHERRY ESSENCE

1 tablespoon olive oil
2 tablespoons chopped shallots
$\frac{3}{4}$ cup Amontillado sherry
$\frac{2}{3}$ cup defatted chicken broth
Salt and pepper

1. Heat oil in a small saucepan over medium heat until hot. Add shallots and sauté, stirring, about 3 minutes, until they are golden.

2. Add sherry, increase the heat, and reduce by a third, about 5 minutes.

3. Add chicken broth, stirring constantly. Continue cooking until broth is reduced by half, about 8 minutes.

4. Season with salt and pepper. Sauce can be stored, covered, in the refrigerator for up to 1 week.

YIELD: About $\frac{1}{2}$ cup

"Sometimes you have to stop and sniff the corks."

Arna Dan Isacsson

CHAPTER 7

WINE SAUCES AND MARINADES

rench cookbooks begin with sauces because they are considered an important part of that cuisine. A sauce can grace a plain ingredient and give it personality or set off an unusual ingredient or elaborate dish.

The sauces in this section vary from marinades to sauces for main-dish ingredients and desserts. Wines are used for flavor and as part of the liquid. When you select a wine to drink with the dish, the sauce is often the determining factor. By adding a particular wine to a sauce, you create the style and taste you want.

WHITE WINE MARINADE

Marinades are a great vehicle for small amounts of leftover wines. White wine gives this marinade a less acidic taste than the usual vinegar. This marinade is great for chicken, turkey, pork, and white-fleshed fish. Thoroughly cook any remaining marinade before serving as a sauce.

$\frac{2}{3}$ cup light- or medium-bodied dry white wine
(Chenin Blanc, Semillon, or dry Riesling)
$\frac{1}{3}$ cup plus 1 tablespoon light olive oil
1 tablespoon fresh lemon juice
1 tablespoon plus 2 teaspoons minced fresh basil or dill
or 1 heaping teaspoon dried basil or dill
1 small green onion, minced
Freshly ground white pepper

1. Blend ingredients together in a 2-cup glass measuring cup. Cover and let the flavors blend for about 15 minutes.

2. Pour over poultry, pork, or fish in a shallow glass dish. Cover the dish and refrigerate while the ingredients marinate. The meat also may be marinated in a thick plastic bag, which should be tightly fastened. Marinate small meat pieces for 30 minutes to 1 hour and larger cuts for 1–2 hours. Drain off the marinade before you broil or grill the meat.

YIELD: Makes about 1 cup, enough for 2–3 pounds of meat

HERBED RED WINE MARINADE

Red wine marinades are best used for red meats and several dark, firm-fleshed kinds of fish, while white wine marinades can be used for red meats or seafood. I like this one for beef, lamb, venison, or duck. Less tender meat cuts can be used, since the marinade tenderizes them. Marinades contain acid, from vinegar or wine, which tends to reduce a meat's moisture-retention capacity during cooking. While the meat might lose juices, it gains in tenderness and taste.

1 cup dry red wine (Barbera, Cabernet Sauvignon, Merlot, Petite Sirah, Pinot Noir, or Zinfandel)

1 tablespoon lime juice

$\frac{1}{4}$ cup olive oil

2 teaspoons Dijon mustard

1 large clove garlic, crushed

Dash Worcestershire sauce

1 tablespoon minced fresh or $\frac{3}{4}$ teaspoon dried thyme leaves

Freshly ground black pepper

1. Combine wine with the remaining ingredients in a small bowl or 2-cup glass measure. Let flavors blend for about 15 minutes.

2. Pour combined ingredients over meat in a shallow glass dish. Cover and refrigerate while the meat is marinating: 1–2 hours for thin cuts, several hours for thicker cuts. The meat may be marinated in a thick plastic bag, which should be tightly fastened. Drain off the marinade before broiling or grilling the meat.

YIELD: Makes about 1$\frac{1}{3}$ cups, enough for about 3–4 pounds of meat

RED WINE BUTTER FOR STEAK

Grilled steaks get a facelift with this delicious red wine butter, which can be prepared in the time it takes to warm the grill. The steaks become extra succulent with the butter sauce. For a variation, I often top the steaks with crumbled blue cheese.

⅔ cup dry red wine (especially Pinot Noir, Zinfandel, Merlot, or Cabernet Sauvignon)

2 tablespoons unsalted butter, softened

1–2 teaspoons chopped fresh rosemary or thyme or ¼ teaspoon dried rosemary or thyme

Salt and freshly ground black pepper

1. Cook wine in a small saucepan over high heat until reduced by half, about 5 minutes. It should have the consistency of a thin syrup. Remove pan from heat.

2. Gradually whisk in softened butter, rosemary, salt, and pepper. The sauce should be creamy in consistency.

3. Pour sauce over the cooked steaks.

YIELD: Makes a scant ½ cup, or 4–5 servings
PAIRING: When served with steak, a Cabernet Sauvignon, Merlot, Zinfandel, or Italian red wine such as Barbera or Barolo

AMONTILLADO-MUSTARD SAUCE

This easy sauce is delicious with many vegetables, such as green beans, broccoli, or cauliflower. I especially love it with grilled salmon, swordfish, or tuna, but it's also great with grilled or broiled chicken. For a sweeter variation that is wonderful with poultry or ham, substitute a sweeter sherry, and use a honey-mustard instead of Dijon. Combine a dry sherry and a whole-grain brown mustard for steaks, lamb chops, or other red meat.

1½ cups Amontillado sherry

⅓ cup Dijon mustard

6 tablespooons cold unsalted butter, cut into 6 pieces

1. In a small saucepan, bring sherry to a boil over high heat; cook until sherry is reduced to ⅓ cup, about 8 minutes.

2. Stir in mustard; reduce the heat to low. Then stir in butter a piece at a time; wait until each piece has been incorporated before adding the next.

3. Serve immediately.

YIELD: About 1 cup

PAIRING: When the sauce is served with poultry or light meat, choose a Chenin Blanc or Chardonnay; with red meat, a Pinot Noir, Chianti, or a light blend.

WILD MUSHROOM SAUCE

Dried porcini mushrooms are great for this recipe because of their intense flavor. I love this sauce over polenta, plain risotto, brown rice, or al dente pasta. It's also excellent with sautéed veal cutlets or chicken breasts. A white wine without oak aging (I used Collio Tocai Friulano) keeps the sauce on the lighter side. I sometimes substitute a light red wine for the white wine and serve the sauce with red meats. This one is thickened with a little roux (butter-flour base) because it gives a better consistency and higher yield than a reduction; increase the roux slightly for a thicker consistency.

3 ounces of dried porcini mushrooms (dried oyster mushrooms and others can be substituted for lighter flavor)

1 cup hot water

1 tablespoon butter

1 small shallot minced (about 2 tablespoons)

1 tablespoon all-purpose flour

$\frac{1}{2}$ cup dry white wine without oak aging

$1\frac{1}{2}$ cups defatted, low-sodium chicken broth, at room temperature (a concentrated vegetable broth may be substituted for a vegetarian version)

2 teaspoons minced fresh thyme or $\frac{1}{2}$ teaspoon dried thyme

Salt and pepper to taste

1. Soak dried mushrooms in hot water for about 20 minutes. Remove mushrooms, reserving the water; dry mushrooms on paper towels, then dice. Strain reserved mushroom water through a paper coffee filter.

2. In a small saucepan, melt butter over low heat, add shallots and diced mushrooms and cook for about 2 minutes.

3. Add flour to shallots and mushrooms, stirring constantly for about 3 minutes.

4. Add wine, chicken broth, and reserved mushroom water, stirring constantly. Add thyme, salt, and pepper and simmer for 20 minutes.

YIELD: About 2 cups

PAIRING: When the sauce is served with polenta or another starch as a side dish, the main course will be the determining factor. Duca Di Salaparuta Terre d'Agala, Italy, is recommended; it's medium-bodied and lively with hints of wild cherry and vanilla. A slightly fuller red wine (Zinfandel or Merlot) would be better with the sauce over veal or chicken.

Note: You can use this recipe to make mushroom soup by increasing the amount of chicken broth to 3 cups, adding 1 cup of vegetables (peas, diced carrots, and onions) in step 2, and stirring in a little half-and-half at the end.

FRESH-TOMATO WINE SAUCE

Plum tomatoes are the best for this sauce because they have great flavor and don't have the seeds and firm skins of larger tomatoes. The sauce will have a better consistency and appearance when the tomatoes are peeled, but when I'm in a rush, I skip that step (the peels give the sauce more texture). This is one of the best tomato sauces because it derives flavor from sautéed shallots and garlic, fresh basil, and a wine rich in fruit. Serve this sauce with polenta, pasta, or rice for a side dish. It's also excellent over chicken or shrimp. Leftover sauce can be covered and stored in the refrigerator for up to five days.

2 pounds plum tomatoes, peeled and quartered

1 tablespoon olive oil

2 shallots, minced

1 large garlic clove, crushed

$\frac{1}{2}$ cup dry, soft, fruity red wine (Frescobaldi Pomino Rosso D.O.C., a blend of Sangiovese, Cabernet Sauvignon, Merlot, and Pinot Noir)

$\frac{1}{2}$ teaspoon sugar

1 tablespoon minced fresh basil or 1 teaspoon dried basil

1 tablespoon Italian parsley, minced

Salt and pepper to taste

1. Plunge tomatoes into a pot of boiling water for about 30 seconds, remove, and rinse them under cold water. The skins should slip off easily. Quarter the tomatoes; set aside.

2. Heat oil in a medium saucepan, add shallots, and cook over medium heat for 2 minutes. Add garlic and cook for 30 seconds.

3. Add tomatoes, red wine, and sugar. Stir and simmer for 15 minutes, until tomatoes are softened into a sauce. Add basil and parsley and continue to cook for 5 minutes.

4. Remove the sauce from the heat and add salt and pepper to taste.

YIELD: About 1 quart
PAIRING: When the sauce is served over polenta, pasta, or rice as a side dish, the wine choice will depend on the main course. A medium-bodied Merlot or Pinot Noir is nice with this. When sauce is served over roasted chicken or boiled shrimp, compatible wines would be lighter reds, such as Chianti, Gamay Beaujolais, or Grenache.

WINE-FRUIT NECTAR SAUCE

The right dessert sauce can perk up puddings and pound or sponge cake, which then can be topped with frozen yogurt. This sauce combines a semidry white wine with fruit nectar, honey, and mint. Rosemary or lemon basil may be used as an alternative herb. Add soft fruit for a bit of thickness and chunk. Experiment with the wine and the nectar, and you're bound to find several favorites.

$\frac{3}{4}$ cup fruit nectar (apricot or peach nectar are good choices)

1 tablespoon honey

$\frac{1}{4}$ cup semidry white wine

1 teaspoon lime juice

2 tablespoons chopped fresh mint leaves or 1$\frac{1}{2}$ teaspoons minced fresh rosemary or lemon basil

Optional: $\frac{1}{2}$ cup chopped soft fruit, (peaches, pears, nectarines, and strawberries are great),

1. Combine nectar, honey, wine, lime juice, and mint in a small glass or ceramic bowl, adjusting amounts to suit taste.

2. Stir in fruit, if desired. Spoon over cake or pudding.

YIELD: About 1 cup without fruit; 1$\frac{1}{2}$ cups with fruit
PAIRING: Late harvest Riesling or Moscato

CHAMPAGNE AND CHOCOLATE CREAM SAUCE

Two of my favorite things, Champagne and chocolate, combine to form a love duet of a dessert sauce. This is a good use for a bubbly that's gone flat. Why serve anything but a sparkling wine with a dessert topped with this creation? It's so effervescent—a lively match!

½ cup whipping cream

½ cup half-and-half

⅓ cup demi-sec sparkling wine (leftover is fine)

2 tablespoons honey

6 ounces semisweet chocolate, cut into small chunks

2 ounces bittersweet chocolate, cut into small chunks

1. In a medium-heavy saucepan, heat whipping cream, half-and-half, sparkling wine, and honey over moderate heat until they are just hot. Do not boil.

2. Remove the pan from the heat and quickly whisk in the chocolate until it is melted and smooth. Serve over vanilla or strawberry ice cream, pound cake, angel food cake, or berries. The sauce may be stored covered in the refrigerator for up to three weeks.

YIELD: About 2½ cups
PAIRING: Demi-sec sparkling wine or sparkling rosé

"Champagne is
the wine-lover's luxury."

Jancis Robinson

CHAPTER 8
DESSERTS AND SWEET IDEAS

Some of my friends say that dessert, the final memory of a menu, is the best part of a meal. I have thankfully curbed my youthful passion for rich, gooey sweets, and now favor fruit and chocolate desserts with crisp textures or light, creamy consistencies. My goal in developing these recipes was for desserts with a balance of flavors and textures that use wine as part of the sweetener.

Sweet wines make wonderful flavorings, but they are very rich, so use them with discretion and in small portions. The German Auslese and Beerenauslese, the French Sauternes and Barsac, and the American late harvest Rieslings can be enjoyed alone, since they are desserts unto themselves. Experiment and make your choices.

Wine allows you to create excellent desserts in minutes. Some of the simplest creations are the best. For instance, soak sliced fruits in moscato, port, or sweet Madeira for at least an hour and serve with a sprig of mint and a little frozen yogurt or crème fraîche. For a quick and elegant finale, pour a little demi-sec sparkling wine or Champagne over berries in a footed dessert goblet. A sauce can be made by reducing one cup of sweet wine with one-third cup of sugar until it is syrupy; strain and serve. Here's to sweet endings!

MANGO FANDANGO

This dessert is named for the Fandango, a dance similar to the Lambada and popular in Argentina. I used Moscato from St. Supéry for this dessert because it is less sweet than most. This creation has a rhythmic harmony among the mangos, pistachios, and yogurt. A bit of lime zest and a touch of honey help balance the flavor composition and make beautiful music. Add a sliced banana for a more substantial dessert.

$\frac{3}{4}$ cup Moscato (St. Supéry)

2 large ripe mangoes, peeled and cut into large chunks

$\frac{1}{2}$ teaspoon grated lime zest

$\frac{1}{4}$ cup plain shelled pistachios, chopped

2 cups plain yogurt

About 2 teaspoons honey, to taste (optional)

1. In a small saucepan over medium heat, reduce wine by half (about 5–10 minutes). Remove the pan from the heat and let cool completely.

2. Toast pistachios in oven for 10 minutes or until just golden brown.

2. Combine wine, mangoes, lime zest, pistachios, yogurt, and honey in a medium bowl. Cover and chill. Serve in dessert bowls or over slices of pound cake.

YIELD: 4 servings
PAIRING: St. Supéry Moscato or a late harvest Riesling

NORWEGIAN BAKED APPLES

People who like taffy apples will like this special treat. Gjetost cheese is a Norwegian goat's milk product that is caramel-colored and sweet. When melted, it complements the apples especially well.

4 small red baking apples (Rome Beauty, Jonathan, Macintosh, or Winesap), halved crosswise (not down through stem) and cored

$\frac{2}{3}$ cup grated Gjetost cheese ($\frac{1}{4}$ of an 8.8-ounce box)

$\frac{1}{3}$ cup chopped walnuts

$\frac{1}{3}$ cup dried currants (or raisins)

1 tablespoon brown sugar

$\frac{1}{2}$ teaspoon cinnamon

$\frac{1}{2}$ teaspoon ground cardamom

$\frac{1}{2}$ cup semidry white wine
(Johannisberg Riesling or Chenin Blanc)

Garnish: vanilla frozen yogurt or ice cream

1. Arrange apple halves cut side up in a 9- or 10-inch microwavable baking dish. (Trim the edges if the apples don't quite fit.)

2. In a medium bowl, mix cheese, walnuts, currants, brown sugar, cinnamon, and cardamom. Spoon mixture over apples. Pour wine over apples.

3. Cook uncovered in a microwave for 3 minutes on a high setting. Rotate the pan and baste apples. Cook for another 2 minutes, until apples are tender. Cover and let stand for 5 minutes before serving. Serve with a scoop of vanilla frozen yogurt or vanilla ice cream.

YIELD: 4–8 servings
PAIRING: Demi-sec Champagne or sparkling wine, late harvest Riesling, or Gewürztraminer.

BAKED BANANAS
in Madeira-Raspberry Sauce

Madeira and raspberries join flavor forces with dried apricots and cardamom to transform bananas into a special dessert. Brown sugar and nuts complete the treat. Served warm, with a scoop of ice cream or frozen yogurt for temperature contrasts, it's a dessert you'll start to crave.

1 10-ounce package of frozen raspberries
with syrup, thawed
1 teaspoon lemon juice
$\frac{1}{2}$ cup Madeira
$\frac{1}{4}$-$\frac{1}{2}$ teaspoon ground cardamom
$\frac{1}{2}$ cup diced dried apricots (3 ounces)
1 teaspoon cornstarch
6 small to medium bananas, firm-ripe
4 tablespoons brown sugar
4 tablespoons chopped nuts

1. Preheat the oven to 425°F. Set aside 2 tablespoons of raspberry syrup. Combine raspberries and the rest of the syrup in a small pot with lemon juice, Madeira, cardamom, and apricots. Bring the mixture to a boil, lower the heat, and simmer for 15 minutes, stirring occasionally.

2. Combine cornstarch with the 2 tablespoons of raspberry syrup. Mix well and stir into the hot mixture, cooking and stirring for 2 minutes.

3. Peel bananas and slice lengthwise without cutting all the way through. Arrange in a large, shallow baking dish. Spoon the raspberry mixture down the center of each banana and sprinkle brown sugar over the top.

4. Place on the lowest oven rack and bake until bubbly, about 10 minutes. Watch them carefully so they don't burn.

5. To serve, cut each banana crosswise, then carefully transfer to an individual serving plate. Arrange the quarters like spokes of a wheel. Divide the sauce among the 6 servings and sprinkle with nuts and brown sugar. Serve warm or at room temperature. This is delicious with a scoop of ice cream or frozen yogurt in the center of each plate.

YIELD: 6 servings
PAIRING: Late harvest Riesling, late harvest Gewürztraminer, or sweet Madeira

CRANBERRY-ORANGE BREAD PUDDING
with Sweet Wine

This pudding is rich and satisfying, a perfect cold-weather dessert that is great even in warm weather. The contrast of sweet wine with tart cranberries and the spark of orange peel is comforting and exciting. I soak the dried cranberries in the wine to absorb its flavor. This is a dessert I love, and I am delighted to share the recipe.

1 cup milk

2 cups whipping cream

Grated peel from 1 large orange

2 teaspoons vanilla extract

1 cup sweet white wine, such as late harvest Gewürztraminer

1 cup lightly packed dried cranberries

1 1-pound loaf challah (braided or plain egg bread)

6 large eggs

$\frac{3}{4}$ cup plus 2 tablespoons sugar

$\frac{1}{4}$ teaspoon cinnamon

1. Preheat the oven to 325°F. In a heavy, medium saucepan, heat milk, cream, and orange peel until bubbles appear around the edges. Then add vanilla, wine, and cranberries; cover the pan and set aside for 15 minutes.

2. Trim the bottom crust off bread; cut bread into 1-inch cubes. Put cubed bread in a large jellyroll pan and bake for 10 minutes until barely golden.

3. In a large pot, bring several quarts of water to a boil, then reduce the heat to a simmer.

4. In a large mixing bowl, whisk together eggs and $\frac{3}{4}$ cup of sugar. Whisk slowly into the hot cream mixture. Add bread cubes and thoroughly but gently mix them in. Let soak for 10–15 minutes before transferring to a greased 9x13 glass baking dish.

5. Mix remaining 2 tablespoons of sugar and cinnamon in a small bowl and sprinkle over the pudding.

6. Place the baking dish inside a larger roasting pan and pour the boiling water in the pan so it comes halfway up the sides of the baking dish. Bake for 35 minutes. Remove from heat and let cool. Serve warm or at room temperature.

YIELD: 14–18 servings
PAIRING: Late harvest Gewürztraminer or sweet Madeira

PLUM-SHERRY SHORTCAKES

Two types of sherry do their magic on this dessert, cream sherry adds a sweet and rich dimension to the plum compote, and the drier Amontillado sherry contributes its flavor to the shortcakes. Serve the compote on its own in a bowl topped with a bit of rich yogurt, or spoon it over ice cream or frozen yogurt.

PLUM COMPOTE

1 tablespoon cornstarch

$\frac{1}{2}$ cup water

$\frac{3}{4}$ cup cream sherry

1$\frac{1}{2}$–2 teaspoons minced fresh orange zest

1$\frac{1}{2}$–2 teaspoons ground ginger

1$\frac{1}{2}$ teaspoons lemon juice

$\frac{1}{3}$ cup sugar

3 pounds assorted plums (sweet and tart)

Sherry Shortcakes (see recipe at right)

1. In a small bowl, mix cornstarch with 2 tablespoons water until dissolved. Set aside.

2. In a medium saucepan, combine cream sherry, orange zest, ginger, lemon juice, sugar, and $\frac{1}{4}$ cup plus 2 tablespoons water.

3. Cut plums into quarters, removing pits, and add to saucepan. Bring plum mixture to a low boil, stirring constantly. Simmer for 8 minutes.

4. Stir in cornstarch and water mixture. Bring to a boil over medium-high heat. Reduce the heat and simmer for 2–3 minutes, stirring occasionally, until slightly thickened.

5. Let the compote cool slightly before serving it with shortcakes.

YIELD: 6 servings

SHERRY SHORTCAKES

2 cups unbleached white flour
$\frac{3}{4}$ teaspoon salt
$\frac{1}{4}$ cup sugar
1 tablespoon double action baking powder
$\frac{1}{2}$ teaspoon minced fresh orange zest
$\frac{1}{2}$ stick (4 tablespoons) unsalted butter, melted and cooled
$\frac{3}{4}$ cup whipping cream
$\frac{1}{4}$ cup Amontillado sherry

1. Preheat the oven to 400°F. In the bowl of a food processor, combine flour, salt, sugar, baking powder, and orange zest. Add butter, cream, and sherry, mixing until the mixture is sticky.

2. On a floured board and with floured hands, knead the dough for 1 minute, adding only enough flour to keep it from sticking to the board. With floured hands, pat the dough into a circle $\frac{1}{2}$-inch thick. Use a 3-inch biscuit cutter to cut out 6 circles.

3. Arrange the circles several inches apart on an ungreased cookie sheet. Bake in the center of the oven until golden brown, 12–17 minutes.

4. Remove shortcakes from the oven and cool them slightly. Serve warm or at room temperature. Biscuits may be split open or sliced crosswise, then filled and topped with plum compote. Add optional whipped cream or vanilla ice cream just before serving.

YIELD: 6 shortcakes
PAIRING: Cream sherry or demi-sec Champagne or sparkling wine

STILTON AND PEAR NAPOLEON

The flavors of the fruity and sweet port, pears, salty Stilton, and walnuts make an exciting mix, and the contrast of the soft mascarpone cheese and pears against the crispy phyllo layers give this dessert a lively texture. Assembling this Napoleon requires care; the delicate fillo layers can break easily when spread with the cheese mixture. The result is worth the challenge.

$\frac{1}{2}$ cup toasted walnuts

1 8-ounce container mascarpone cheese

About $\frac{1}{2}$ cup ruby port

1–2 tablespoons honey

2 large very ripe pears (D'Anjou, Bartlett, and Comice are all good choices)

1 stick butter, melted and kept hot

1 box phyllo dough (1 pound or less)

2–3 ounces Stilton, crumbled (Gorgonzola may be substituted)

1. Toast walnuts in 350°F oven for 10 minutes. Cool and grind coarsely.

2. Preheat the oven to 400°F. Mix mascarpone cheese, 3–4 tablespoons ruby port, and honey in a small bowl. Set aside.

3. Slice pears thinly, lay the slices on a plate, and drizzle with the remaining $\frac{1}{4}$ cup ruby port. Let soak while you bake the phyllo dough.

4. Carefully open the box of phyllo dough, unroll the paper-thin sheets, and remove 3 sheets. Roll up the remainder, seal tightly in a plastic bag, and store in refrigerator or in the freezer if not previously frozen.

5. On a large, clean cutting board, brush 1 sheet of phyllo dough lightly with melted butter. Top this with a handful of walnuts. Stack and repeat with the other two phyllo sheets, topping each with walnuts.

6. Transfer to a cookie sheet and carefully cut the phyllo dough into 12 even pieces. Keep the phyllo together rather than spreading the pieces out. Bake until they are golden brown, about 5 minutes. Phyllo burns easily, so check it after 4 minutes. Remove the cookie sheet from the oven and let it cool on a rack.

7. To serve, arrange one square of phyllo on each of four individual dessert plates. Top each portion with one-quarter of the pear slices, add another phyllo square, and spread one-quarter of the cheese mixture over it. Cover each with one-quarter of the blue cheese and one of the remaining phyllo squares. Serve immediately.

YIELD: 4 servings
PAIRING: Ruby or tawny port, sweet Madeira, or sweet sherry

LOW-FAT CHOCOLATE MINI-MUFFINS
with Strawberry-Port Sauce

These chocolate mini-muffins are like tiny cakes, and a trio of them on a plate with the Strawberry-Port Sauce makes a lovely light dessert. They are more cake-like than true breakfast muffins, and the batter might also be used in different ways to make filled muffins or chocolate pancakes that would make a great brunch item.

5 ounces semisweet or bittersweet chocolate

3 tablespoons milk

$\frac{1}{2}$ cup whole wheat flour

$1\frac{1}{2}$ cups unbleached white flour

2 teaspoons baking soda

2 tablespoons softened butter

$\frac{3}{4}$ cup plus 2 tablespoons sugar

3 eggs

$1\frac{1}{3}$ cups extra-strong coffee, cooled

$\frac{2}{3}$ cup ruby port

Strawberry-Port Sauce (see recipe at right)

1. Preheat the oven to 350°F. Lightly grease the mini-muffin pans.

2. In a small pan over very low heat, melt chocolate and milk, stirring constantly. Remove from the heat and set aside.

3. In a small bowl, mix whole wheat and white flours and baking soda; then set aside. In a separate bowl, combine coffee and ruby port.

4. Using an electric mixer, cream butter and sugar. Add eggs and beat well. Then add chocolate mixture.

5. Alternate adding the flour mixture and the coffee mixture to the batter, 3 parts flour and 2 parts liquid.

6. Use a glass measuring cup to pour the mixture into the muffin pans until the cups are $\frac{3}{4}$ full.

7. Bake the muffins for 10–15 minutes, until a cake tester comes out clean. Remove them from the oven and cool in the pans for 5 minutes before removing. If the muffins stick, use a grapefruit knife to loosen the edges. When they have cooled, serve them three to a plate with sauce spooned around.

YIELD: 60 mini-muffins or 20 servings
PAIRING: Ruby port (which reinforces the flavor in the dessert), sweet Madeira, or a demi-sec Champagne or sparkling wine

STRAWBERRY-PORT SAUCE
1 pound ripe strawberries, chopped
$\frac{1}{4}$ cup ruby port
2 tablespoons honey

1. In a small saucepan, combine strawberries, ruby port, and honey. Simmer until the fruit is soft, about 8–10 minutes.

2. Remove the sauce from the heat and let it cool. Serve as is or purée it in a blender or food processor.

YIELD: About 2 cups

JOAN'S CHOCOLATE MARSALA CAKE

This delicious cake was created for this book by pastry chef Joan Hersh, proprietor of "A Matter of Course," a Chicago catering firm. The cake is moist and rich from the Marsala and coffee, with sparks of orange peel. After decorating it with the icing and white chocolate, you'll be proud to serve it at a special dinner party.

$\frac{1}{4}$ cup dry instant coffee

1$\frac{1}{4}$ cup water

$\frac{3}{4}$ cup Marsala

2 sticks (1 cup) unsalted butter, softened

1$\frac{1}{2}$ cups sugar

1 teaspoon vanilla extract

Grated peel of 1 orange

$\frac{1}{2}$ teaspoon orange extract

3 eggs

1 teaspoon baking soda

$\frac{1}{2}$ teaspoon salt

6 ounces unsweetened chocolate, melted and slightly cooled

2 cups plus 2 tablespoons unbleached flour

Chocolate Icing (see recipe on page 126)

1. Preheat the oven to 325°F. Grease and flour a 9-inch, 2-piece tube pan.

2. In a 2-cup glass measure, dissolve coffee in $\frac{1}{3}$ cup warm water. Add cold water to the 1$\frac{1}{4}$-cup mark (or use 1$\frac{1}{4}$ cups extra strong brewed coffee). Add Marsala.

3. Cream butter in a large mixing bowl. Add sugar, vanilla, orange peel, and orange extract and beat at medium speed for 2 minutes. Scrape the sides of the bowl and add eggs, beating until smooth. Add baking soda, salt, and chocolate. Continue beating until

the chocolate is incorporated. Scrape the sides and beat for an additional 30 seconds. Using a low-speed setting, alternate adding flour and coffee-marsala mixture, 3 parts flour and 2 parts liquid, scraping the sides as needed. Beat well for 1 minute. Pour the batter into the tube pan and smooth the top with a rubber spatula.

4. Bake in the center of the lower shelf for about 1 hour or until a wooden pick or cake tester comes out clean. The cake shouldn't bake for more than 1 hour, 15 minutes.

5. Remove the cake from the oven and let it cool for 20 minutes before removing the outer pan. Then let the cake cool on the center tube until it is cool to the touch. Refrigerate the cake until it is cold and remove the tube by sliding a sharp, thin knife between the cake bottom, the pan, and around the tube.

6. Prepare Chocolate Icing (see page 126).

7. Ice the cake and chill for a few minutes until the icing is firm before adding the White Chocolate Drizzle (see page 126) or serving. It is best eaten at room temperature.

CHOCOLATE ICING

3 tablespoons unsalted butter

2 tablespoons Marsala

$\frac{3}{4}$ teaspoon vanilla extract

1 cup plus 2 tablespoons confectioners' sugar, sifted

1 tablespoon cocoa

1. In a small saucepan, melt butter over low heat. Add Marsala and vanilla and stir until hot. Over medium heat, add the sugar and cocoa, whisking constantly. Cook for 3–4 minutes, bringing the mixture to a boil.

2. Place the cake on a wire rack over a jellyroll pan to catch drips.

3. Remove the icing from the heat and immediately brush it onto the cake using a heat-proof pastry brush, covering all sides.

WHITE CHOCOLATE DRIZZLE

2 ounces white chocolate chips or bulk white chocolate, chopped

1 teaspoon corn oil

1. Combine chocolate and oil in a microwavable dish. Heat, loosely covered, in a microwave oven on medium until the chocolate is melted, 1–2 minutes.

2. Stir chocolate until it is smooth, then drizzle the icing over the cake with a fork. Let it harden for a few minutes before serving.

YIELD: 1 9-inch cake, serving 8–12

PAIRING: Marsala, late harvest Gewürztraminer, Moscato, Black Muscat, or Hungarian Tokaji (Tokay)

CHAPTER 9
CHEESE AND WINE HARMONY

Wine and cheese make a harmonious culinary marriage, with endless varieties and combinations. While the two generally go well together, some types of cheeses are not complementary with certain wines. Some cheeses are too mild and light for robust wines, and others are too strong for light wines. It does take a bit of tasting and experimenting to discover what you really prefer.

The following cheese and wine guide can assist you in trying some mutually enjoyable pairings. This list includes most of the more popular cheeses sold in this country. Find a retail cheese and wine shop with a good selection and knowledgeable staff or a supermarket with good cheese and wine departments.

It's difficult to improve upon the traditional and regional wine and cheese matches of European countries. One traditional match is English Stilton with tawny or vintage port from Portugal. Some regional examples are the full red Rhône wines with local chèvres and lighter Spanish Rioja red wines (Bordeaux-type) with firm local cheeses, like Manchego.

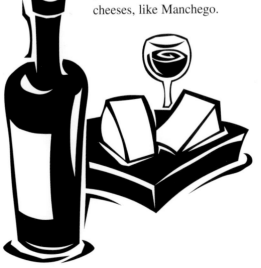

When planning a cheese board or a cheese and wine tasting party, select some cheeses from each category, from soft to firm. Soft and soft-ripened cheeses include Brie and Camembert; the semisoft category is comprised of those ripened in different ways and has the unctuous Port Salut, Muenster, and most blue-veined cheeses; firm includes cheddar and Emmentaler; and the hard group (usually grating cheeses) includes asiago and Parmesan. For a well-rounded cheese board, consider cheese flavors from mild to medium-strong or strong. For instance, Brie, Emmantaler, blue-veined, St. Paulin, and a specialty cheese such as spiced Norwegian Nokkelost or herbed Danish saga, make an interesting group. Avoid the ultraripe, strong cheeses, since they mask a wine's flavor. When serving a fine wine, match it with mild cheese. Serve cheese at room temperature with plain crackers or bread. Add a cheese spread, too (see Chapter 1, pages 13–14).

Think through the wines that would be best matches for the cheeses you are serving and select one or several for each category. For an educational cheese- and wine- tasting party, label the cheeses with brief descriptions and list suggested wines. Have notepads and pencils at the ready so guests can remember favorite matches.

APPENZELLER. This cheese from Switzerland uses wine and spices in the maturation. Best with medium-bodied whites such as Semillon and light reds such as Grenache, Gamay Beaujolais, Valpolicella, and Swiss Neuchâtel.

BEL PAESE. Its slight tart flavor has a hint of a bitter aftertaste, and its soft, creamy texture is cut by an acidic wine such as a dry sparkling wine, Pinot Blanc, Sauvignon Blanc, dry Riesling, or a dry, light red, such as Valpolicella.

BLUE (BLEU). This American cheese is a challenge to match because it is salty and pungent. Only young fruity whites and reds (Riesling, Gamay), big reds (Fortant de France Cabernet Sauvignon or some Zinfandels or Petite Sirahs) and sweet (Sauternes, late harvest Riesling) can stand up to it.

BRIE. Called the queen of cheeses, it is soft-ripened with a white, thin rind and runny center. In its young and mild state, it has a subtle tangy taste and seems perfect with most wines, including the fine, vintage French red Burgundies. In its older and more robust state, it is especially compatible with fruity, young red wines like Gamay Beaujolais, some rosés, Chiantis, and soft Merlots.

CAMEMBERT. In its mild, delicate state, this soft-ripened cheese with a white, thin crust and creamy center has a tangy taste and is especially good with an acidic wine (Pinot Blanc, Sauvignon Blanc, or brut Champagnes). In its mature state, its flavor is fuller, more bitter, and best with full reds (Cabernet Sauvignon).

CHEDDAR (includes New York Herkimer). It comes in mild to sharp. It goes well with light- to full-bodied reds or whites; the milder, younger variety goes with younger, lighter-bodied wines. Even some sweeter wines (late harvest Gewürztraminer, Madeira, or port) are good with the sharp type.

CHÈVRE. This goat's milk cheese varies in flavor and consistency from mildly tangy, soft, and creamy to sour and peppery. It is happy with complex red wines (Cabernet Sauvignon, some Pinot Noirs, Syrah, South African Pinotage, and medium- to full-bodied Italian red wines, such as Nebbiolo).

EDAM. One of the most adaptable, agreeable cheeses, it has a wholesome, mellow taste and a semihard texture. Equally enjoyable with wines from dry whites (Sauvignon Blanc) to light- to medium-bodied reds (Gamay Beaujolais, Bardolino, or Pinot Noir).

EMMENTALER. This is the true Swiss cheese and the model followed by manufacturers of "Swiss cheese." Emmental Français is the type made in France. Complemented by light white wines (Swiss Neuchâtel is the native match; also Riesling, Gewürztraminer).

FONTINA. Creamy and semifirm with a sweet, delicate, butternut taste. The true Fontina Val d'Aosta has a brush-like, pale yellow rind. Best with softer whites (Chenin Blanc, Semillon, or Riesling; some lighter styles of Chardonnay) and with lighter reds (Pinot Noir, Valpolicella).

GORGONZOLA. This blue-veined Italian cheese is successful with young red wines (Grenache, Gamay Beaujolais, Pinot Noir, or some fruity Zinfandels) and some sweet wines (port, late harvest Riesling, or extra dry or sec Champagne).

GOUDA. Similar to Edam, this versatile cheese is mild with a rich, satisfying flavor and semihard texture. It is delicious with wines from dry white (Sauvignon Blanc) to light, fruity red (Gamay Beaujolais, Bardolino) to fuller dry red (many Pinot Noirs, Zinfandels, or Cabernet Sauvignons).

GRUYÈRE. This sweet-nutty firm cheese with a hint of bitterness is enjoyable with full-bodied white and red wines (Chardonnay, Cabernet Sauvignon).

JARLSBERG. This fine Norwegian cheese (resembles Swiss-style) is complemented by light white wines (Swiss Neuchâtel, Semillon) as well as dry white wines (dry Riesling, Sauvignon Blanc) and lighter reds (Pinot Noir).

MUENSTER. This soft cheese has a simple, light, fresh taste and is a fine companion with dry white wines, (Sauvignon Blanc, light-style Chardonnays), and vivacious, fruity, young reds (Gamay Beaujolais, Grenache), and Mediterranean-style rosés.

PARMESAN. Served thinly shaved or in thin slices, this salty, hard Italian cheese is delightful with crisp, dry white wines (Pinot Grigio, Sauvignon Blanc) and with light to fuller reds (Bardolino, Nebbiolo, or Cabernet Sauvignon).

PORT SALUT. Creamy and firm, it is mild and buttery when young and more bold-flavored, but not strong, when mature. Good with lighter styles of dry whites (Chardonnay) and the livelier reds (Gamay Beaujolais, fruity Zinfandel).

PROVOLONE. Some dry whites have enough backbone to stand up to this cheese with its sharp flavor (some Sauvignon Blancs, Chardonnays). Usually best with big red wines (Amarone, Syrah).

ROQUEFORT. This strong, salty, blue-veined sheep's milk cheese will overpower many subtle, fine wines. It needs fruity whites and reds (Riesling, some fruity Zinfandels), big reds (Cabernet Sauvignon), or sweet wines (tawny or vintage ports). The French mate this native cheese with Sauternes (sweet).

STILTON. This internationally loved, British, blue-veined cheese has mellow undertones of a Cheddar and a smooth, velvety consistency. The classic match is tawny or vintage ports or big Burgundies (Pinot Noir). Some sweeter wines such as an extra dry or sec Champagne also work.

APPENDICES

MENUS FOR WINE AND FOOD

Menu planning is a key step in making your event successful. Good planning will help ensure an efficient, enjoyable occasion. To help with your party preparations, here are several different menu ideas. Most of the recipes and wine pairings are drawn from previous chapters. Some dishes can be prepared in advance, especially for the wine tasting menu for 12, so you aren't overwhelmed on the day of your party.

ELEGANT DINNER FOR 4

Bay Scallops with Snow Peas and
Dill Crème-Fraîche (p. 86)
Chardonnay (without or with little oak aging)

Roast Rack of Lamb Provençal (p. 68)
Cabernet Sauvignon

Boiled New Potatoes with Olive Oil

Asparagus with Lemon Butter

Green Salad with Sprouts and Cherry Tomatoes and
Lime Vinaigrette

Cranberry–Orange Bread Pudding
with Sweet Wine (p. 116)
Late harvest Johannisberg Riesling

Crisp Butter Cookies

Demitasse or Espresso

DINNER FOR 6

Asian Green and White Salad (p. 22)
Dry Riesling or Sauvignon Blanc

Risotto with Leeks and Fennel (p. 46)
Chardonnay or Sauvignon Blanc

Steak with Mushroom-Merlot Sauce (p. 58)
Merlot or Cabernet Sauvignon

Plum-Sherry Shortcakes (p. 118)
Cream Sherry or demi-sec Champagne or sparkling wine

Coffee or Tea

WINE-TASTING DINNER PARTY FOR 12

When serving this menu for a dozen people, it's best to get eight to 10 bottles of wine to offer a variety. Consult your trusted wine retailer and request some good values.

Balance the wine tasting so that a Champange or sparkling wine is served first, then progress to dry whites or fortified aperitif wines, and on to light reds and heavier reds. Sweet wines should be saved for last. Have at least four wine glasses per guest, unless you are prepared to rinse out glasses between courses. Provide pitchers of water, water glasses, and notepads so guests can evaluate their wine samples.

For the wine tasting, a basic tulip-shaped glass is best. Pour about one-fourth of a serving per tasting. Encourage your guests to try a sip of each wine first without food, then sample each again with food to taste how their perception of a wine changes with food.

The simplest wine tasting can be planned around a simple cheese board laden with a variety of crackers or bread. When you want to get more elaborate and prepare a meal, consider the following menu.

As you gain confidence with your wine-tasting galas, start to experiment. For example, plan a wine tasting that compares one varietal from several countries or wineries within a region or a vertical tasting with one wine of several different vintages, progressing from youngest to most mature.

Port–Blue Cheese "Cake" Appetizer (p. 12)
Port, Champagne or sparkling wine, Semillon, or
Gamay Beaujolais

Polenta Triangles (p. 18)
Duca Di Salaparuta Columba Platino, Italy, for the toppings with olives, pepper, and proscuitto. For the tomato and mushroom sauces, the same producer's medium-
bodied Terre d'Agala

Three Greens Goat Cheese Salad
with 1-2-3 Vermouth Dressing (p. 25)

Bread

Vineyard Pasta with White Wine Sauce (p. 38)
Pinot Grigio, Sauvignon Blanc, or Gamay Beaujolais

Pork Grenache Stew (p. 32)
Grenache, fruity Zinfandel, or Pinot Noir

Low-fat Chocolate Mini-Muffins with
Strawberry-Port Sauce (p. 122)
Ruby port (which reinforces the flavor in the dessert),
sweet Madeira, or demi-sec Champagne
or sparkling wine

Appendix B
AFFORDABLE WINES FROM AROUND THE WORLD

I've been compiling this list for quite a long time, adding wines I like as I taste them. My criteria for selecting these include affordable price range and characteristics to be good food wines (generally not much oak aging, not high alcohol, and not huge tannins). Some are over $20 a bottle, but most are under $16, and a good number are between $4 and $10 a bottle—great finds for both drinking and cooking.

Jug wines are not listed, but some are especially good for cooking. When you need a large quantity of wine for a recipe or when you have a small supply of a better wine that you'd prefer to drink, then cooking with a jug wine makes sense.

Vintages are listed because they are the ones I've sampled and are available at press time, but vintages are not an important concern here. These are reputable producers who market reliable wines. When a vintage isn't up to standard, the winery will not produce the wine that particular year.

This list is not intended to be comprehensive. I have tasted and enjoyed numerous wines, but have narrowed the selection drastically to be able to include wines from various countries.

CHARDONNAY

Beringer Chardonnay 1990 (CA): Ripe apples and citrus flavors; rich, long finish; elegant and full bodied.

Etchart Cafayate 1994 (ARGENTINA): Elegant, well-balanced; nice varietal aroma; fruity, pleasant aftertaste.

Fetzer Barrel Select Chardonnay 1994 (CA): Full varietal flavor intensity with layers of creamy vanilla, tropical lemon fruit, butterscotch, and toasty oak; smooth, rich, and complex.

Fleur Ducap Chardonnay 1995 (SOUTH AFRICA): Pale color; slightly buttery aroma with hints of pear, peach, and spice, hints of toasty vanilla; medium- to full-bodied.

Landmark Overlook Chardonnay 1994, 1995 (CA): These two vintages are similar with golden yellow color; ripe fruit tastes of peach, apple, and pear; floral, honey overtones. Made with a wild yeast fermentation that produces wine of great complexity and length that is versatile with food.

St. Supèry Chardonnay 1994 (CA): Aromas of apples and melon with hints of French oak; full-bodied, creamy in texture with long finish.

Wyndham Estate Bin 222 1995 (AUSTRALIA): Full-flavored, definite Chardonnay taste; melon-like fruit; rich, elegant with subtle oak.

CHENIN BLANC

Chappellet 1004 Old Vine Cuvée Chenin Blanc (CA): Crisp; tart apple and citrus aromas and flavors; melon undertones.

Llano Estacado Chenin Blanc (TX): True to varietal characteristics, with melon and tropical fruit aromas; semidry; light, delicate with soft fruit fragrance.

Lynfred Winery 1995 Chenin Blanc (IL): Very pale straw color; forward varietal aromas of grapefruit with a lovely floral bouquet; crisp fruit flavors of grapefruit and lemon.

GEWÜRZTRAMINER

Hugel Gewürztraminer 1993 (FRANCE): Heady perfume of varietal grape that leads to full, round flavors; dry finish. Historically one of the best houses for Alsatian wine.

Palmer Winery Gewürztraminer 1995 (NY): Varietal aromatics; trace of residual sugar maximize fruit qualities.

Schlumberger Gewürztraminer Fleur de Guebwiller 1993 (FRANCE): Intense fruit in aroma and taste, but dry and spicy; typical varietal characteristics.

PINOT BLANC

Trimbach Pinot Blanc 1994 (FRANCE): Sturdy with good acidity and light body. One of the best Alsatian values.

PINOT GRIGIO

Neirano Oltrepo Pavese D.O.C. 1994 Pinot Grigio (ITALY): Pale yellow, fruity and medium-bodied. From Oltrepo Pavese in the south of Lombardy region.

Sterling Vineyard Sterling Collections Pinot Grigio 1994 (CA): Among the more delicate, fresh, and light Pinot Grigios; dry.

RIESLING

Castell Müller-Thurgau Trocken 1994 (GERMANY): Hearty, lively, elegant wine with a perfumed aroma and ample body.

Dr. Frank's Johannisberg Riesling 1995 (NY): The 1994 vintage was served by the White House; the 1995 vintage is served by American Airlines in first class. Great typical fruit in aroma and flavor.

Forster Ungeheuer Riesling Spätlese 1994 (GERMANY): Floral and fruit aromas; sweet, balanced finish.

Hogue Johannisberg Riesling 1995 (WA): Lively, medium-dry with fine acid structure; ripe fruit aromas of peach, apricot, hints of honeysuckle and anise; refreshing with finish reminiscent of peach and honey.

Rooiberg Rhine Riesling 1994 (SOUTH AFRICA): Semidry, spicy and fruity; balanced fruit and acidity. When young, it's fresh and floral. When mature, it will be complex and spicier.

SAUVIGNON BLANC

Buena Vista Lake County Sauvignon Blanc 1995 (CA): Light yellow-green color; aromas of peaches, pears, and tropical fruit; rich, full taste; refreshing finish.

Cakebread Cellars Sauvignon Blanc 1995 (CA): Crisp and slightly acidic; varietal aromas of grapefruit and lemon; flavors of citrus and melon.

Clos du Bois 1994 (CA): Nice acidic balance with hints of grapefruit, grass, and vanilla.

Kenwood Sauvignon Blanc (CA): Lighter with good body and fruit showing; no characteristic varietal herbaceousness.

Matanzas Creek Winery Sauvignon Blanc (CA): Layers of rich citrus, pineapple, melon, and fig flavors; delicate; crisp backbone; lingering finish; not very grassy.

Viansa Sauvignon Blanc (CA): Well-balanced fruit and acid; not very grassy.

Viña Errazuriz Sauvignon Blanc 1995 (CHILE): Crisp and fruity balance; lightly perfumed; fresh citrus; long finish.

CABERNET SAUVIGNON

Atlas Peak Cabernet Sauvignon 1991 (CA): Intense blackberry and cassis aromas and flavors; some oak and moderate tannins.

Burgess Cellars Cabernet Sauvignon Vintage Selection 1992 (CA): Well-balanced and approachable; moderate tannins and good varietal characteristics.

Cakebread Cellars Napa Valley, Cabernet Sauvignon 1993 (CA): Well-developed aromas of black cherry, plum, and cedar; flavors similar with touch of toasty oak and vanilla; full-bodied, easy drinking wine with ideal balance.

Caliterra Cabernet Sauvignon 1994 (CHILE): Aromas and flavors of blackberry, vanilla and spice; fruit is accented by a hint of oak and soft tannins for a full, warm palate and finish.

Chateau St. Michelle Cabernet Sauvignon 1993 (WA): Classic Bordeaux style; dry, full-bodied and complex with sweet wood, ripe cherry aromas; cassis flavors; long finish.

Cinnabar Cabernet Sauvignon 1993 (CA): Limited production and one of the best produced by this winery. True varietal character shines through without the excessive vegetal qualities of some.

Miguel Torres Cabernet Sauvignon 1993 (SPAIN): Firm and well-structured; aromas of berries and plums; clean, fresh, lingering aftertaste.

Wyndham Estate Bin 444, Cabernet Sauvignon 1994 (AUSTRALIA): Rich, deep color; full well-blended berry fruit flavors integrated with oak, which adds complexity.

BARBERA

Louis M. Martini Barbera 1991 (CA): Aroma and flavors of cherry fruit; light, approachable version of this varietal.

GAMAY BEAUJOLAIS

Georges Duboeuf Beaujolais (FRANCE): Fruity, fresh red wine; lively acidity; drink very young. Can be served chilled.

GRENACHE

Julian Chivite Rosé (D.O. Navarra), Garnacha 1995 (SPAIN): Intense strawberry flavor; good acidity balanced with fruit; body of a light red wine.

Torres, Gran Sangre De Toro 1991 (SPAIN): Rich generous aroma, plums and strawberries, spice from oak, hint of licorice. Mediterranean-style; earthy, with soft tannins.

MERLOT

Bethel Heights Vineyard Pinot Noir Flat Block Reserve 1994 (OR): Unfiltered; powerful fruit; beautifully perfumed; elegant.

Buena Vista Carneros Estate Merlot 1994 (CA): Big fruit flavors of cherry, plum, blackberry, and soft tannins; hint of licorice and black pepper in nose; lingering aftertaste.

Columbia Crest Merlot 1993 (WA) Appealing ripe berry and cocoa notes complement the wine's perfumed nose. Fresh red raspberry flavors are followed by a soft, toasted oak finish.

Fortant De France White Merlot 1994 (FRANCE): Pale pink with deep violet reflections; intense nose of ripe raspberries; lively acidity balanced by sweetness.

Markham Vineyards Merlot 1994 (CA): Loaded with fruit, especially ripe grapes; aromas of herbs and berries; rich flavor. The winery also makes an excellent Cabernet Sauvignon.

PINOT NOIR

Eikendal Pinot Noir 1994 (SOUTH AFRICA): Light in texture with a ripe fruity decadence; smooth and flavorful; gently drinkable.

Gloria Ferrer Carneros Pinot Noir 1994 (CA): One of the best Pinot Noirs I've had. Rich in ripe fruit; plum, strawberries, luscious; full of aroma and flavor. Harvested from the sweetest and most mature grapes.

Monticello Estate Pinot Noir, 1993 (CA): Rich red color; aromas of vanilla and toast; flavors of black cherry and strawberry; long, silky finish; soft tannins.

Vins De Suisse Dôle Des Monts (SWITZERLAND): Switzerland's most popular red wine; light with aroma of ripe fruit; silky texture.

SANGIOVESE

Lungarotti Sangiovese 1994 (ITALY): Firm aromas; flavors typical of this grape varietal; dry; medium-bodied; bright, fruity, fresh tasting with a bit of spice, a little oak; medium tannins; approachable style.

SYRAH

Joseph Phelps Vin du Mistral Syrah 1993 (CA): Firm tannins; spicy, licorice-like aromas; hints of blackberry and mocha in the bright fruit flavors.

Navarro Correas, Mendoza Syrah 1992 (ARGENTINA): Intensely red; scent of violet and cassis; full-bodied red wine with characteristic flavors; velvety finish.

Penfolds Bin 128 Coonawarra Shiraz 1993 (AUSTRALIA): An elegant, crimson-red wine; spicy pepper flavor; ripe berry fruit; soft vanilla oak tannins.

Stellenryck Shiraz (SOUTH AFRICA): Full-bodied, well-structured.

ZINFANDEL

Blaauwklippen 1990 Stellenbosch (SOUTH AFRICA): Moderately tannic with medium body and fruit; black fruits dominate with hints of leather, spice; forceful flavors for well-seasoned hearty fare.

Haywood Estate Zinfandel 1993 (CA): Rich blackberry and black pepper spice aromas and flavors plus raspberries balanced with oak; full-bodied.

J. Fritz Winery Zinfandel 1994 (CA): Forward fruit, well-balanced and structured with medium amount of tannin; cherries and raspberries in flavors and finish; food-friendly.

Rosenblum Cellars California Zinfandel, Vintners Cuvée XIII (CA): First cuvée representing the superb 1995 harvest. Zesty fruit, moderate oak; soft yet satisfying.

DESSERT AND FORTIFIED WINES

Blandy's J.B. Rainwater Madeira (PORTUGAL): Medium sweet and well-balanced;versatile enough for drinking before or after meals.

Cockburn's Special Reserve Port (PORTUGAL): Full-bodied, medium sweet ruby port with a hint of dried plums.

Dow's Fine Ruby Port (PORTUGAL): Casked for a maximum of three to four years. Full and rich with sweetness; ideal for after-dinner sipping. In France, drunk as aperitifs.

Dow's Fine Tawny Port (PORTUGAL): Aged in wood three to 10 years. Lighter port than the Fine Ruby; amber color. Best served chilled as an apéritif or after dinner with dessert or a creamy cheese.

Intorcia Marsala Superiore D.O.C. (ITALY): Fortified, sweet red wine; great for cooking, adds depth of flavor.

Justino's Medium-Dry Madeira (PORTUGAL): Medium-rich, golden; some sweetness and dry finish; all-purpose wine for before or after meals; also available dry and medium-sweet.

Noilly Prat Dry Vermouth (FRANCE): Intense, like liquid herbs.

Noilly Prat Sweet Vermouth (FRANCE): Strong, concentratred; herbal and sweet; in style of Italian sweet vermouth.

Osborne Amontillado Sherry (SPAIN): Light in color, body and flavor; dry, but rich and tasty; deep tone and aftertaste.

Palmer Winery Select Harvest 1994 (NY): Dessert wine with lavish exotic aromas and flavor intensity from a rare concentration of flavor and sugar, coupled with selective harvesting of the best fruit.

Pedro Ximenez 1827 Sherry (SPAIN): Very dark color. Sweet, resembles prune juice; nutty, deep tones and aftertaste. Excellent, rich and full; blockbuster sipping wine.

St. Supèry Moscato 1993 (CA): Sweet white wine; richly floral; excellent balance of sweetness and acidity.

Tokaji Wine Trust Company Sátoraljaújhely, Tokaji (HUNGARY): This dessert wine of Hungary is intensely sweet.

CHAMPAGNE AND SPARKLING WINES

Ariel Blanc de Noirs (CA): De-alcoholic; dry, nice body and stream of bubbles; pleasant grape aromas and flavors; one of the best of its type.

Chateau Frank 1989 Brut Champagne (NY) Very dry, full-bodied, well-structured sparkling wine. Similar to French-style Champagne. Has been served at the White House.

Cristalino Brut Cava (SPAIN): Clean, crisp, drier cava style; honey and citrus flavors with toasty spicy aromas; dry, elegant, refined; one of the best bargains.

Domaine Carneros Brut 1991 (CA): Typical Taittinger style of refinement and finesse. Brilliant straw-gold color with strands of persistent pinpoint bubbles. Subtle, rich ripe fruit of melon and crisp citrus with toasty, vanilla notes.

Domaine St. Michelle Blanc de Blanc Sparkling Wine (WA): Lighter, more supple and rounded than a brut.

Jepson Blanc de Blanc Champagne 1991 (CA): Light apple aromas and flavors; yeasty and spicy notes; creamy texture; dry finish.

Laurent Perrier Brut NV (FRANCE): Yeasty, with flavor tones of apples and lemons; refreshing citrus finish.

Roederer Estate Anderson Valley Brut (CA): Dry; good body with finesse and depth. Complex; nice streams of tiny bubbles.

Scharffenberger Cellars Brut Rosé (CA): Lovely coral color; made primarily from Pinot Noir grapes and the fruit flavors come through; light toastiness; creamy with crisp finish; a stylish bubbly.

BLENDS AND OTHER NOTABLE SELECTIONS

Benziger Estate Tribute Red 1991 (CA): A classic Bordeaux blend from 20 different flavor blocks on the Sonoma Mountain estate with intense fruit and great complexity. It is a special blend of estate Merlot, estate Cabernet Sauvignon, Cabernet Franc, Petit Verdot, and Malbec.

Boutari Santorini 1994 (GREECE): Pale yellow with rich, pleasant aromas of ripe fruit. Wine has a crispy acidity. Well-balanced with good structure; aromatic, long-lasting aftertaste.

Caves Du Chateau D'Auvernrer Neuchâtel 1995 (SWITZERLAND): Crisp, light wine with an almost imperceptible sparkle and floral bouquet. No wood aging.

Duca Di Salaparuta Terre D'Agala 1993 (ITALY): Vibrant ruby-red color, fragrant nose spiced with wild cherry and hint of vanilla; substantial acidity. Exuberant; medium-bodied; good balance.

Frescobaldi Castello di Nipozzano Chianti Rufina Riserva D.O.C.G. 1992 (ITALY): Deep ruby; elegant combination of black fruits and oak aromas; ripe fruit on the palate balanced with some oak; fine tannins in finish.

Masi Amarone Classico Superiore D.O.C. 1991 (ITALY): Deep ruby coor, intense aromas of ripe marascoa cherries, rich and warm. Great structure with medium tannins.

Middelvlei Pinotage 1991 (SOUTH AFRICA): Intense ruby color; plummy aroma with faint oaky vanilla scents. Medium bodied with big fruit taste and massive tannic structure; capable of aging many years.

Penfolds Organic Clare Valley Shiraz-Cabernet Sauvignon 1994 (AUSTRALIA): Full bodied; deep red with purple hues; dark plum, chocolate, ground coffee, and oak flavors; ripe spicy blackberry aromas.

Zonnebloom Grand Soleil 1991 (SOUTH AFRICA): Blend of three French varietals: Chardonnay, Sauvignon Blanc and Chenin Blanc producing an herby, grassy, dry wine with nuances of oak.

BASIC HOME CELLAR

Creating your own wine cellar at home is a great way to have different wines on hand for special and everyday occasions and to save money. Having your own collection is convenient when you want wine with a meal and when you entertain on short notice. Buying wines at your leisure means you can stock up on your favorites when they are on sale or buy wine by the case, cutting costs considerably. Buying wines with great aging potential also will give you the added pleasure of expectation in waiting for the uncorking and tasting.

Location, motion, and temperature are important to your wines. Wine should be kept in a cool place, preferably at 55°– 60°F. A constant temperature is best for allowing wines to mature properly, so store wines away from heaters and the kitchen. A north or interior wall of a house often has the coolest temperature, while a south or west wall often has the hottest. Movement disrupts the maturing process, so keep your wines in an out-of-the-way place away from elevators, stairs, and moving equipment.

Ideally, wines are kept in a temperature-controlled room designed specifically for wine storage, but you can easily create your own cellar, even if you don't have a spare room. All you need is some space in a cabinet, closet, or even a bookshelf. Ready-made wine racks and storage systems, from inexpensive plastic or wooden racks to very elaborate temperature- and humidity-controlled cabinets, are available to fit just about any space requirement.

Once you have put the wines in your cellar, avoid moving them around, especially the older wines. Wines with corks should rest on their sides so the corks stay wet, preventing air from leaking in and ruining the wine. Wines with plastic stoppers can be placed in an upright position. Store wines with the bottoms facing out so you can see the sediment, which indicates that the wine is aging correctly.

Keep in mind that the temperature close to the floor is lower than the temperature higher up. Sparkling wines age best in a cooler environment, so you may wish to stack wines in the following order, starting with the closest to the floor: sparkling, white table, red table, appetizer, and dessert.

Once you have a few bottles of wine, you may wish to keep a cellar book of the name of the wine, vintner, year, dealer, quantity, price, dates purchased and used, as well as any tasting notes.

The selection should depend on your personal tastes and those of your guests. In planning a good balance of wines, select several sparkling wines, from brut to demi-sec (if you like the sweeter style); dry to semidry white table wines, such as Chardonnay, Sauvignon Blanc, and Riesling; dry to fruity red tables wines, such as Merlot, Cabernet Sauvignon, Pinot Noir, Zinfandel, and Gamay Beaujolais; and several aperitif and dessert wines—perhaps vermouth, port, and sherry. Below are some general guidelines for cellaring:

REDS   Cabernet Sauvignons often last five years or longer. Some Pinot Noirs and Barberas can be stored for several years. Reds mellow with age, and some Bordeaux take up to 10 years to mature. Good Bordeaux to store in a cellar include 1982, 1985, 1986, 1988, 1989, and 1990.

WHITES   Gewürztraminers, Chardonnays, Sauvignon Blancs, and white Burgundies will last for several years. Many whites, however, taste best when consumed soon after their release.

SPARKLING   The bubbles disappear soon after the wines are opened, but the flavor remains for several days if the bottle is recorked and kept refrigeratored or in a cool place. Leftover, flat sparkling wine may be used in the Champagne and Chocolate Cream Sauce (see p. 109).

APERITIF AND DESSERT WINES   Sherries, Madeiras, ports, and other fortified wines can be stored at 60°–70°F for a few years without losing their flavor. Drier sherries, however, taste best when fresh. Muscatels, sweet dessert sherries, and ports develop fuller flavor after aging for years. Once opened, the higher alcohol wines can be stored at cool room temperature. Lower alcohol wines, such as some Moscatos, need to be treated like table wines. Store them with a VacuVin cork or transfer them to smaller bottles without air space. Flavored wines are not designed for storage.

Appendix D
TABLESIDE TIPS
AND CARING FOR WINE

After you've selected the wine you want to serve, open it, and examine the cork. If the cork is firm and moist, pour some wine into a clear glass to observe its color and aroma. If the wine looks and smells agreeable, then go ahead and enjoy a taste. If the cork is moldy or the wine smells sour, air may have gotten into the wine and ruined it. This wine should be discarded or returned to the store.

Most wines should be served from their bottles. Only old wines with sediment need to be decanted. When serving wine to guests, be sure that the label is showing—not hidden by a napkin.

If the wine is to be served chilled, refrigerate it for one-half hour before serving. Instead of putting it into an ice bucket filled with only ice, mix the ice with water and a little rock salt to give the wine a quick chill, then remove the bottle when the wine reaches its proper serving temperature. RapidIce®, available in many liquor stores, comes in handy to quick-chill bottles.

When it comes to wine openers, there are several main styles and a few options. The two main elements to look for in a corkscrew are good leverage and a good worm (the part that screws into the cork). Never buy a corkscrew whose point is exactly in the center, as this bores into and weakens

the cork. Corkscrews whose point lines up with the spirals grasp the cork better and allow for an easier release. The traditional waiter's type, similar to a Swiss Army knife with a hinged corkscrew that must be pulled out, is always handy to have around. Winged openers with their superior leverage are easy to use, but my favorite is the plastic Screwpull® by Le Creuset, which comes in an attractive clear plastic stand and cover. The hinged cutter slices through the outer foil wrap over the cork and the pliable outer covering of the long corkscrew clamps around the bottle neck, so you can easily hold the bottle while turning the corkscrew.

Champagne, which should be served very cold, requires special care when opening. Point the cork away from you and your guests. Undo the wire hood, then grasp the cork between your thumb and forefinger so the cork is in your palm. Twist and lift, turning the bottle until the cork pops.

The flavor of wine is diluted by contact with air and heat, so use table wines and sparkling wines as soon as you can after opening. Get a VacuVin® for leftover wine or pour leftover wine into a smaller bottle so there is no airspace and recork. When you plan to use leftover wine for cooking, a thin layer of olive oil added to the surface prevents oxidation and preserves the quality of the wine.

Without air, wine can be stored at a cool room temperature for about two weeks. With airspace, store it in the refrigerator overnight. If the wine is several days old and has lost its full charm, use it for cooking, unless it's spoiled or has an off taste.

GLASSWARE

Though it may seem as if the sizes and shapes of wine glasses are limitless, all you need to get started is a set of clear, tulip-shaped glasses. Look for a glass that is dishwasher safe and at least 6 inches high, with an inward-curving bowl that holds 8–9 ounces. The number of glasses you need depends on your storage space and how many people you entertain.

When you are ready to expand your selection, you may wish to purchase champagne flutes, sherry glasses, and large bowl glasses, which are often used for red wine. If your budget allows, you can even get glasses designed for a specific grape variety.

Appendix E
GLOSSARY OF WINE TERMS

ACIDITY The tart, sharp flavor of wine caused by its natural grape acids. A favorable characteristic in moderate amounts, it should not be confused with sourness or astringency. Decreases with age.

A.O.C. Stands for Appellation d'Origine Contrôlée. Government-controlled designation indicating that the wine comes from a particular place in France.

APERITIF From the French word meaning appetizer. Refers to wines served before meals.

APPELLATION Denotes that the wine comes from a specific location and is typical of wines from that region.

AROMA The grapy fragrance of a wine.

BALANCE A pleasant, harmonious flavor achieved from the right proportions of a wine's sugar content, acidity, and other odor and taste elements.

BARREL-FERMENTED Refers to a method of fermenting wine in barrels, adding complexity and aging potential.

BODY The substance of the wine, body is related to the alcohol content: The more alcohol, the bigger the body.

BOUQUET The smell of a wine as it ages and develops.

BRUT A standard French term that usually designates the driest Champagne or sparkling wine of a vintner. "Brut" (very dry) is drier than "Extra Dry" (slightly sweet) but is slightly sweeter than "Nature."

CLASSICO Means that the wine comes from the heartland of a production area. Usually refers to Italian wines.

CLEAN Refers to a wine that is refreshing and leaves a sense of cleanliness in the mouth and nasal passages.

COLOR One of the most distinctive characteristics of wine. It can vary from gold to amber in a white wine and from ruby to garnet in a red wine.

CORKY Refers to a smelly, woody odor of wine. The result of tainting from a defective cork.

CRÉMANT Non-Champagne sparkling wines in France.

CRU An estate in France. The term also indicates that a high-quality vineyard produced the wine.

DECANTING The process of slowly pouring an older wine into a different container to separate the wine from any sediment at the bottom of the bottle.

DEMI-SEC Designates a sweet variety of sparkling wine and Champagne.

DESSERT WINES Sweet or partially sweet wines. Some are 17 percent to 20 percent alcohol.

D.O. Denóminacion de Origen; meaning a wine of a particular place or region in Spain.

D.O.C. Denominazione di Origine Controllata; meaning a wine made from a particular place or region in Italy.

DRY Refers to the lack of sweetness in wine.

EISWEIN A wine made of frozen grapes, resulting in a higher concentration of grape sugars.

ESTATE-BOTTLED Refers to wine that was grown, produced, and bottled at the same vineyard.

EXTRA DRY A misnomer, since it designates a slightly sweet style of sparkling wine or Champagne.

FERMENTATION The process through which yeast action converts grape sugars to alcohol and carbon dioxide.

FINO A light, dry, or very dry fortified wine from Andalusia, Spain. Some sherries are fino or dry.

FLINTY An austere taste or smell detectable in wines grown in stony soil. It supposedly resembles the smell of flint when struck with steel.

FORTIFIED A wine that has had brandy or grape spirit added to increase its alcohol content. Fortified wines last longer than nonfortified table wines.

FRUITY Refers to a wine that has a grape fragrance and flavor.

FULL Refers to a wine that has a pleasant, strong flavor and smell.

LIGHT Refers to a wine that has a low alcohol content.

MELLOW Refers to a soft, sweet wine; usually red.

MÉTHODE CHAMPENOISE A classical method of Champagne production in which a secondary fermentation takes place in its bottle. Also known as "Méthode Classique."

MUSTY Refers to an odor similar to decaying wood. A musty-smelling wine has been spoiled.

NATURE A French term with the same meaning as brut: No sweetener has been added.

NOSE A term referring to the overall smell of the wine, including fragrance and bouquet.

OAK A traditional type of wood, dating back to the Romans, that is used in wine storage barrels. The older the oak, the less impact it has on the flavor of the wine.

OXIDATION The process in which wine slowly changes and becomes spoiled by oxygen.

QUALITÄTSWEIN "Quality Wine" in Germany.

QUALITÄTSWEIN MIT PRÄDIKAT "Quality Wine with Distinction" in Germany.

RICH Refers to a full-bodied, flavorful wine.

RISERVA A term describing greater merit and barrel in wines from Spain, Portugal, Italy, Chile, or Argentina.

ROBUST Refers to a sturdy, hearty wine.

SEC Refers to sparkling wine and Champagne. Means "medium sweet," which is confusing because sec is a French word meaning "dry." Secco is Italian and used in similar fashion.

SEKT A sparkling wine from Germany.

SPÄTLESE German word referring to particularly ripe grapes.

SPUMANTE Italian sparkling wine, often slightly sweet and fruity.

STILL WINE Wines from which all the carbon dioxide has been removed. The opposite of sparkling wines.

TABLE WINE Mostly dry wines. They are 10 to 14 percent alcohol, less than dessert wines.

TAWNY The brown, orangish color to which port wine changes when aged in a barrel.

VARIETAL Refers to both the grape and the wine from which it is made.

VIN DE TABLE French term for table wine.

VINIFERA The species of grape from which the vast majority of wines are produced.

VINIFICATION The process of turning grapes into wine, which includes fermentation, clarification, and aging.

VINTAGE The harvesting, crushing, and fermentation of grapes from a specific year into wine. Commonly used to refer to a season's yield of wine.

INDEX